PRAISE FOR *THE FULLNESS OF THE GROUND*

"Judith Blackstone has the rare capacity to guide readers into a direct experience of embodied, nondual realization. Not only that, she offers clear wisdom teachings that enable us to bring the fruits of this awakening—love, vitality, clarity, openness—alive in all facets of our life. Highly recommended."

TARA BRACH
author of *Radical Acceptance* and *Trusting the Gold*

"Judith Blackstone continues her pioneering work in the field of embodied nonduality by guiding us to the direct experience of our fundamental ground in and through our body that is both spacious and substantial, empty and radiantly full, individuated and undivided from the whole of life. An important, groundbreaking work marked by clear insight, subtle sensitivity, and practical guidance. Highly recommended!"

JOHN J. PRENDERGAST, PHD
author of *The Deep Heart* and *In Touch*

"A rare guide for truth lovers interested in having their eyes, arms, and hearts open. Blackstone sets forth her guidance and deep insights into varying realizations of nonduality, essential emptiness, and universal presence—with great care for their outcomes and fulfillment. Her Realization Process offers liberation to identities, emotions, and experiences that have been unconscious, suppressed, and denied, as their encounters with presence enfold them in timeless, vivid Being. For readers interested in both transformative power and self-refinement."

MUKTI
teacher of *The Self in Full Bloom*, co-teacher of *The One of Us*

"This groundbreaking book gives us a map and practical tools to begin to embody awakening by discovering this is an already inherent potential within us. Judith is a wonderful, clear, and sensitive guide for combining the most precious ancient wisdom with modern psychological ways to heal. Rather than trying to create a positive part of us to counteract our difficult emotions, we learn here to access fundamental support with simple shifts of perception and grounding meditations that release chronic patterns of suffering. I have met many of Judith's students who have clearly benefited from this brilliant and unique approach, which is now available to us all in *The Fullness of the Ground*. Highly recommended!"

LOCH KELLY
author of *The Way of Effortless Mindfulness* and *Shift into Freedom*

"In *The Fullness of the Ground* Judith Blackstone offers a beautifully written and masterful guidebook that provides us with a clear, contemporary, and exquisitely outlined path of wisdom and practices for recognizing and embodying our innate Wholeness amid our daily lives, whereby we can experience true connection and intimacy within ourselves and with the world around us. This is a gem of a book that lays a firm foundation for realizing and embodying our birthright of both psychological integration and spiritual awakening. Both profound and practical, Blackstone reveals the road we all must travel to embody our potential as fully alive, awake, and authentic human beings. A must-read!"

RICHARD MILLER, PHD
author of *iRest Meditation* and *The iRest Program for Healing PTSD*

the
FULLNESS
of the ground

ALSO BY JUDITH BLACKSTONE

*Trauma and the Unbound Body: the Healing
Power of Fundamental Consciousness*

*Belonging Here: A Guide for the Spiritually
Sensitive Person*

*The Intimate Life: Awakening to the Spiritual
Essence in Yourself and Others*

*The Enlightenment Process: A Guide to Embodied
Spiritual Awakening*

*The Empathic Ground: Intersubjectivty and
Nonduality in the Psychotherapeutic Process*

the
FULLNESS
of the ground

A Guide to Embodied Awakening

JUDITH BLACKSTONE, PHD

sounds true
BOULDER, COLORADO

Sounds True
Boulder, CO 80306

This book is not intended as a substitute for the medical recommendations of
physicians, mental health professionals, or other health-care providers. Rather,
it is intended to offer information to help the reader cooperate with physicians,
mental health professionals, and health-care providers in a mutual quest for op-
timal well-being. We advise readers to carefully review and understand the ideas
presented and to seek the advice of a qualified professional before attempting to
use them.

Published 2023

Cover design by Huma Akhtar
Book design by Linsey Dodaro and Meredith Jarrett

Printed in the United States of America

BK06609

Library of Congress Cataloging-in-Publication Data

Names: Blackstone, Judith, 1947- author.
Title: The fullness of the ground : a guide to embodied awakening /
    Judith Blackstone, PhD.
Description: Boulder, CO : Sounds True, 2023. |
    Includes bibliographical references.
Identifiers: LCCN 2022053456 (print) | LCCN 2022053457 (ebook) |
    ISBN 9781649630445 (paperback) | ISBN 9781649630452 (ebook)
Subjects: LCSH: Duality (Logic) | Opposition, Theory of. | Spirituality. |
    Self-realization--Religious aspects. | Whole and parts (Philosophy) |
    Perception. | Consciousness.
Classification: LCC BC199.D8 B543 2023 (print) |
    LCC BC199.D8 (ebook) | DDC 160--dc23/eng20230413
LC record available at https://lccn.loc.gov/2022053456
LC ebook record available at https://lccn.loc.gov/2022053457

10 9 8 7 6 5 4 3 2 1

Contents

Practices

Introduction

What does it mean to become whole? What does it mean to feel oneness with other people and with your surroundings? Are these just New Age clichés or empty promises of some alternative reality? In this book I show that we have the potential within our own body and within our ordinary reality to become more unified within ourselves as individuals and at the same time to transcend our individuality and uncover an experience of actual oneness with everything around us.

This unity of oneself and one's surroundings is called nonduality. In the following chapters I describe the experience of nondual realization, of what it feels like to know one's whole self—to be able to think and feel and sense all at the same time—and the extraordinary experience of whole-body openness, of the felt continuity between our own being and our environment. I also illustrate the depth of contact and intimacy with ourselves, with other people, and with our surroundings that emerges with this unity. And I point to the ease and happiness that we can uncover within our bodies that is strangely independent of circumstances. This enduring happiness is not a vacuous, detached state. Nor does it interfere with the richness of life or with our natural tendencies to grieve our losses, feel anger at tyranny, or fear when there is actual danger. Yet when we awaken to and embody nondual reality, this sense of well-being is always there, at our foundation, supporting us and helping us to help others.

Throughout these pages, I will show how to access this wholeness and oneness, for it is easily accessible and well within our reach. Through methodical and gentle refinement of our perception and a deepening of our inward contact with ourselves, we can discover what has been here all along. We can uncover our birthright as human beings.

This book is a guide to embodied nondual realization and its profound effect on our senses; on our ability to love, think clearly, and feel pleasure; on our enjoyment of our own authentic existence; and on our connection with other living beings. The method offered here for achieving nondual realization differs from many traditional and contemporary approaches. It is not solely a technique for emptying the mind or expanding awareness. Rather, it teaches the opening of our whole body and being to the experience of oneness. This transforms all of our experience, deepening and refining our capacities for awareness, emotion, and physical sensation.

The practices included here provide the best way I know to convey the message of our spiritual potential. They stem from an approach to embodied nondual awakening called the Realization Process, which I developed and have taught for four decades. The Realization Process is a series of attunement practices for inhabiting your body and uncovering a subtle ground of being, an undivided fundamental dimension of consciousness that you can experience pervading your body and environment as a unity. The Realization Process also includes practices for releasing trauma-based constrictions from the body, which I described in my last book, *Trauma and the Unbound Body*, as well as movement practices and relationship practices to help heal and deepen our intimacy with other people. This book focuses specifically on the Realization Process practices for nondual, spiritual awakening. If you are new to these practices, I hope you will try them out. For this is not a book about metaphysical claims or spiritual beliefs. It is a book about experience. And although I attempt to describe that experience, my effort can only consist of two-dimensional words until you experience their meaning for yourself.

In the Realization Process, nondual realization is experienced as the laying bare of fundamental consciousness. When we uncover it, we experience that our own body and our surroundings are pervaded by and made of this same undivided expanse of consciousness. We recognize it as our primary nature, the fundamental ground of our own being, and at the same time, the ground of our experience of the world around us. Again and again, people who discover this unified dimension say, "Amazing! I have never been here before!" and yet they have not moved at all. They are just perceiving themselves and their world more clearly from a perspective that reveals an underlying unity, a subtle luminosity, and a sense of truth, of immediacy, in all of their experience.

Fundamental consciousness is seen and felt as unbroken, unwavering space that pervades all of the changing content of our experience. Our own body and the world around us appear to be both substantial and made of space at the same time. But this space is not just emptiness. It is experienced as empty, sheer transparency and at the same time as being full of quality-rich presence. When we know ourselves as this ground, our own body and everything and everyone in our environment appear simultaneously to be made of emptiness and radiant presence.

An important consequence of fundamental consciousness pervading both our body and our environment is that we arrive at an experience of our internal wholeness that coexists with our experience of unity with everything around us. Far from eradicating the sense of our individual existence as many nondual approaches attempt to do, with the realization of fundamental consciousness we mature as unique human beings while at the same time experiencing undivided continuity with other people and with our surroundings. Pervading our body, fundamental consciousness emerges with the impact of authenticity, a sense that we have finally come home to ourselves, that we are finally who we really are.

The first part of this book begins with an explanation of nonduality, especially as it is understood and experienced in the Realization Process. It then looks at some of the prevalent views of other nondual teachings regarding the existence or nonexistence of the self and the effect of nondual realization on emotional suffering, desire, agency, and our ability to think and feel.

Throughout this book, I draw on nondual teachings from Buddhist and Hindu[1] traditions to support and contextualize the Realization Process. Although I have studied with masterful teachers in the

Zen Buddhist and Tibetan Buddhist Dzogchen and Mahamudra paths, as well as the paths of Advaita Vedanta, Bhakti yoga, and Kashmir Shaivism, I have never considered myself to be a Buddhist or a Hindu. Growing up in a strictly atheist home, I was left on my own to explore my early spiritual intuitions and experiences. The Realization Process developed out of that exploration. However, my own spiritual unfolding and the development of my work have been profoundly influenced by the Asian nondual teachings. Because it is beyond the scope of this book to offer a detailed or nuanced portrayal of these vast, complex spiritual philosophies, I have only included those teachings that have been relevant to the development of the Realization Process.

I have great respect for people who commit to one spiritual path and in doing so help to keep their chosen tradition intact. Many of my students feel that there is no conflict between their traditional spiritual path and the Realization Process and have found it helpful to integrate the Realization Process practices with those of their chosen tradition. But I also believe that the wisdom with which these traditions illumine the understanding and cultivation of our human nature belongs to all of us. The insights of these religions can touch our innermost core, with each one touching that core from a slightly different angle. This is how I have held the Buddhist and Hindu nondual teachings that I have been fortunate to encounter.

All of the world's great religions arose in a specific part of the world and in a specific time in human history and carry with them that time and culture's beliefs and customs. Many of these traditions spread throughout the rest of the world and endured into later historical eras where they maintained their deep roots and original form but also produced offshoots of new religions. These newer religions sometimes arose from a critique of the older religion's limitations and sometimes from an adaptation of the older religion's tenets to the time and culture of the new religion. When Hindu and Buddhist teachings arrived in the West, they met with the existing psychological knowledge that had developed in Western culture along with other aspects and attitudes of Western society. This produced the New Age movement of spirituality in which many hybrids of psychology and Asian philosophy emerged.

I regard most traditional and New Age metaphysical assertions to be speculative, and readers may be surprised that I am critical of some of the Buddhist or Hindu teachings or at least the prevalent interpretations of these teachings. This criticism is based on my work as a psychotherapist and spiritual teacher where I have observed the harm that some interpretations of the teachings can cause; for example, when people attempt not to exist or not to have emotions because their spiritual teacher advised them that enlightenment requires that kind of suppression.

Now that we have access, through global transportation and communication, to all of the world's spiritual systems, we can see that they sometimes disagree with one another. For me, in this post-postmodern philosophical era, I find it necessary to live with metaphysical uncertainty. It seems to me that there are some things that we simply cannot know. That is not a criticism of religious traditions but a contemporary perspective on them. But this uncertainty does not interfere with our ability to realize the nondual ground of our being. And the experiences of realization that are described, especially in the nondual Asian traditions, can help guide, support, and affirm our present-day nondual realization.

The second part of this book presents the Realization Process path to realizing oneself as fundamental consciousness. It describes the defining attributes of this fundamental ground of our being so that we can recognize and continue to open to this primary aspect of ourselves. It also includes instructions for the main spiritual practices of the Realization Process, some that returning readers will have found in my previous books, and some that have not been published before.

The third section of the book presents ways to bring the Realization Process practices into our daily lives, while walking, speaking, and relating with other people. It includes practices for couples to experience how meeting as fundamental consciousness can deepen, balance, and enhance their connection with each other. All of the practices can help us stabilize in nondual realization as an ongoing transformation rather than a temporary peak experience.

Fundamental consciousness is beyond our habitual, constructed templates of experience, but it is not just ideas or mental constructs that impede our opening to it. For most of us, the realization of fundamental consciousness as one's own nature cannot be achieved with a simple mental shift. Nor can we just decide to settle into this ground and find ourselves there. Our limiting grip on ourselves is embedded and bound in the tissues of our body. We need to make deep contact with ourselves within our body, to become conscious throughout our body, and to let go from the innermost core of our body to free our authentic nature from the chronic patterns that obscure it.

Most importantly, we do not need to suppress any aspect of our experience to realize nonduality. Fundamental consciousness encompasses and pervades all of our perceptions, thoughts, emotions, and sensations. As fundamental consciousness, we experience the ground of our being as both unwavering stillness and full of the movement of life at the same time.

Part 1

WHAT IS NONDUALITY?

1

Two Views of Nonduality

t is all one!" has been the exclamation of mystics throughout the ages. It is a pinnacle, an ultimate revelation of spiritual aspiration. Yet spiritual oneness has been understood, expressed, and taught quite differently within different traditions. It has been understood as oneness with God, as an ecstatic merging with the vibrations of the universe, as a loss of self in the other, and as a gaining of Self that encompasses all otherness. It has been taught as a stopping of one's thought and emotions, even as the disappearance of all perception of form, and it has been taught as the most fluid freedom of thought and feeling, as the sharpest perception of objects and events. All of these perspectives and more have been offered by different teachers, spiritual texts, and traditions as nonduality.

As I will describe in this chapter, most of the teachings on nonduality can be divided into two main categories: those that recognize an essence or ground of being that is the basis of the experience of oneness and those that claim that there is no ground, only the constantly changing flux of experience. Tibetan Buddhist scholars have neatly classified the first as "empty of other" (Tibetan: shentong) and the second as "empty of itself" (Tibetan: rangtong).[1] These two points of view also appear in both ancient Greek and contemporary Western philosophy, but it is the Tibetan Buddhists who have produced a neat and explicit division between the two. Although the main divisions within Hindu philosophies concern the relationship of ultimate reality to our material world, there too we can find a distinction in the teachings about whether or not there is a knowable, fundamental ground.

I am not presenting these two views in order to be argumentative. Within Tibetan Buddhism this is a complex subject, at times involving political and doctrinal concerns and also giving rise to attempts to integrate the two views, saying that they are really the same or that they go to the same endpoint. But of greater interest to me and, I believe, of relevance to the contemporary spiritual seeker, is that these are really two distinct perspectives. They each offer a different understanding of our essential nature and how to uncover it. However, especially among New Age teachers in the West today, one or the other view is often taught simply as nonduality. This means that the spiritual seeker has no options and can only accept their teacher's particular view. But given the choice, some people will naturally be drawn to go more deeply into the experience of a world that is empty except for the constantly changing flux of experience, and others will be drawn, as I have been, to explore more fully a unifying ground that pervades and encompasses this constant change.

The differences between traditional conceptions of nonduality are important for the spiritual student. They have significant bearing on the direction and goals of our spiritual realization, such as whether nonduality means that we still have emotions, whether we can embody nonduality, whether we can have relationships in nonduality, and even whether we continue to exist as distinct human beings.

It may be easy for us, with all the world's traditions at our fingertips, to get lost in a labyrinth of spiritual teachings, riddled with conflicting signposts. I have included a description of these two categories of nonduality in this book partly to help guide the reader in the direction they wish to go and also to explain why the Realization Process is aligned with the shentong "empty of other" perspective. The purpose of the practices presented here is to uncover fundamental consciousness as the foundational ground of our being. This ground can be called the essence of our being because it is experienced as unchanging and unmoving. Unlike all of the changing content of our experience, it is not constructed or imagined—it is revealed as we refine and deepen our attunement to ourselves.

As the most subtle potential of our own being, nondual realization can be nurtured within a religious structure, cultivated without a traditional structure, or even discovered spontaneously. For most of us, even if we have had a spontaneous revelation of oneness, we need some sort of guidance, some sort of practice in order to experience nonduality as our stable, ongoing reality. Many of these practices can be found within religious traditions, especially within the structures of Buddhism and Hinduism. However, the understanding and method that I present in this book are not part of a religious tradition. They are based on my own realization and on the needs and discoveries of my students. However, many of my students have used the Realization Process practices to deepen their realization within their own religious tradition.

Like most contemporary Western nonduality teachers, I have spent many years in the study and practice of Asian spiritual traditions, mainly the Mahamudra and Dzogchen teachings of Tibetan Buddhism and Zen Buddhism and the Hindu teachings of Advaita Vedanta and Kashmir Shaivism. They have had a profound influence on me and, I believe, on much of the spiritually awakened elements of our society. What I found especially useful in these traditions was the confirmation and enrichment of the spiritual experience that I had privately treasured, in its nascent form, since my childhood. As a child, I glimpsed what appeared to be a numinous presence in the sky and trees in my backyard. As an adult, during the intense inward process of healing myself of a back injury that had stopped my career as a dancer in its tracks, I found this subtle consciousness again. I no longer experienced it as a presence separate from myself but as the foundation of my own being. But I felt that I recognized it from my childhood, as if it had always been there and was now more clearly revealed.

The experience of fundamental consciousness can seem very odd. It reveals one's own being and one's environment as both substantial and made of empty, luminous space at the same time. In the Buddhist and Hindu literature, I found descriptions of this odd experience that seemed to resemble my own, as well as guidance for deepening and stabilizing that realization. I felt assurance that an experience that seemed more subtle and more personal to me than my own breath has been known, described, and valued for thousands of years.

Having had some experience of fundamental consciousness emerge during my process of self-healing, I was more interested, from the start of my spiritual path, in accounts from those teachings that pointed to a fundamental ground of being than those that denied it. I searched the spiritual literature for any mention of this ground.

Although the rangtong "empty of itself" perspective is more widely known in the West than the shentong, we find references to a unified ground of consciousness in both the Advaita Vedanta and Kashmir Shaivism philosophies of Hinduism and in some teachings, or some interpretations of the teachings, within Zen Buddhism, Taoism, and the Mahamudra and Dzogchen philosophies of Tibetan Buddhism. As you will see in the quotes below, this ground is called by a variety of names, including Buddha-nature, Self, pure consciousness, primordial mind, and the clear light of wisdom mind. The literature of these spiritual traditions also contains many firsthand accounts by spiritual sages expressing delight in knowing themselves as this spiritual foundation. Even though these accounts come from different traditions with different and even conflicting philosophical and metaphysical systems, the experience they depict appears to be recognizably the same.

Here, for example, are two quotes from the fourteenth-century Tibetan Buddhist teacher Longchen Rabjam, also known as Longchenpa. He wrote, "Within the spacious expanse, the spacious expanse, the spacious expanse, I Longchen Rabjam, for whom the lucid expanse of being is infinite, experience everything as embraced within a blissful expanse, a single nondual expanse"[2] and "Mind itself—that is, the nature of awakened mind—is pure like space, and so is without birth or death . . . it is unchanging, without transition, spontaneously present, and uncompounded."[3]

And this is from Shankara, the ninth-century teacher of Advaita Vedanta: "I am the Supreme Brahman which is pure consciousness, always clearly manifest, unborn, one only, imperishable, unattached, and all-pervading and non-dual."[4]

This final quote is from a root text of the Kashmir Shaivism philosophy: "The individual mind intently entering into the universal light of foundational consciousness sees the entire universe as saturated with that consciousness."[5]

For me, the similarity of these descriptions of a pervasive, luminous consciousness at the base of one's own mind and identity, affirms that it is an experience available to all of us. We can each reach this subtle foundational ground of our being; it is our actual nature, our innate potential as human beings.

CHOICES

The complexity within Asian religion was first illustrated to me by an event in my early spiritual training. It was 1981 and I was living at a Zen monastery in upstate New York. The residents, around thirty of us, were huddled around a clunky small-screened television. We were watching videos of a series of lectures that had recently been given by the Dalai Lama on his first tour of the United States.

He was mesmerizing. Although he was speaking in Tibetan, a language unfamiliar to all of us there, we were pulled as one into the concentrated thought and powerful love that he conveyed in his voice and presence. Yet I found what he was saying, via his translator, to be less than compelling. It had a great deal to do with tables and how they were comprised of different parts that could themselves be divided into different parts, and it concluded finally that there was really no such thing as a table, beyond the meaning attributed to this assemblage of parts by human beings.

There was no essence of tableness within the table. I later heard this articulated as the "nonfindability of inherent reality in objects and persons from their own side." This was not really breaking news to my postmodern sensibility. I had grown up knowing that all of our experience is filtered through our subjective templates and interpretations. That, as Gertrude Stein put it, "There is no there, there." I also understood that as a method of spiritual practice, this was meant to help us achieve a sense of nongrasping and lead to a more direct, vivid experience of life, relatively unobscured by mental elaboration.

However, I felt instinctively that this deconstruction of the objective world had little bearing for my own spiritual path. It did not shed light for me on the experience of numinous presence that I had felt in the sky as a very young child or that I later felt in my body when I was a young dancer or that I was now beginning to experience pervading not only my body but the world around me. After months of intensive meditation practice at the monastery, I was experiencing an intriguing sense of weightlessness, of transparency that seemed to coexist with the substance of the world. If we were going to talk about tables, I wanted to know why the table seemed to be made of empty luminous space while still being a table. It was my intimation of and my attraction to the mysterious transparency of the world that had brought me to live at a Zen monastery.

As the Dalai Lama ended his talk, I felt let down. I even thought, "Well, so much for Buddhism." Then he said, "This that I have just explained to you is a very profound Buddhist philosophy. If it interests you, you should dedicate the remainder of your life to trying to understand it. But if it doesn't interest you," and here he looked straight at us with a mischievous smile, "Buddhism has many other philosophies that might interest you more."

After his long, passionate discourse on what I would later learn was the perspective of his own Gelugpa sect, I found his ending on this democratic note to be moving as well as instructive. It pointed out to me that people are instinctively drawn to particular philosophies, that we are each more compatible with some spiritual approaches than others. We need to follow our own lights to get to the path that feels right, and to do that, we need to understand the differences between the various paths and philosophies. This is especially true today when every possible point of view is available, and when spiritual teachings are often promoted with persuasive commercial skill.

NONDUALITY PERSPECTIVES

Nonduality has become a popular teaching in the contemporary spiritual field. Although there are varying, conflicting perspectives and practices now offered as nonduality, these teachings also have important elements in common. They all view human beings as intrinsically endowed with the means to understand or even to realize the primary nature of reality. For most nondualists, ultimate reality is accessible through a deepening and refining of our own experience. I once heard an Indian teacher say, "First you are in the light, then the light is in you, then you and the light are the same." Nondual realization is this third stage of understanding.

The difference between the two main categories of nondual teachings is in what they consider to be ultimate reality. This distinction affects the types of practices employed to realize nonduality and the beliefs and values that the spiritual aspirant will cultivate in order to succeed on that path.

In the rangtong "empty-of-itself" view, the approach to realization is usually cognitive or analytical, like the Dalai Lama's mental exercise of taking apart the table. It is the cultivation of an understanding of the impermanent, constructed nature of everything we experience. It emphasizes the principle of codependent origination—that everything we experience arises from previous causes. It also seeks to eliminate mental elaboration, such as the attribution of names and associations to objects, by understanding the arbitrary, subjective nature of this mental elaboration. Because of the impermanent, cause-dependent, compounded and subjectively interpreted nature of objects and people, it considers them to be illusory, as having no findable, true existence.

Cultivating this perspective can help us let go, to some extent, of our defensive grip on ourselves. If we do not really exist, what is there to protect? With this understanding, we can allow the river of life to flow and change. Stripped of mental elaboration, we can experience a bright, clear display of phenomena, an unclouded alertness to the present moment. One of the main goals of this practice is to overcome the suffering that comes from attachment, from trying to grasp on to what is essentially impermanent.

Here is a quote from the early Buddhist Bahiya Sutta that states this clearly:

> This time the Buddha relented and said, "Well then Bahiya, you should train yourself like this: whenever you see a form, simply see; whenever you hear a sound, simply hear; whenever you smell an aroma, simply smell; whenever you taste a flavor, simply taste; whenever you feel a sensation, simply feel; whenever a thought arises, let it be just a thought. Then 'you' will not exist; whenever you do not exist, you will not be found in this world, another world, or in between. That is the end of suffering."[6]

A common practice in Advaita Vedanta is a mental exercise called "not this, not this" or neti neti, in which the practitioner carefully recognizes, "I am not my sensations, not my emotions, not my thoughts." For some teachers and their students, this practice leads to where the Buddhist cognitive practices lead, with nothing left, nothing real.

However, this same Advaita Vedantic practice is sometimes taught as leading to an understanding that there is a dimension that we really are, after eliminating our identity with our changing thoughts, feelings, and sensations. This is a ground of pure (unmodified) consciousness or Self that is not identified with the mentally constructed ideas of oneself or with the flux of emotions, sensations, and thoughts. It leads to the shentong "empty-of-other" view of an unmodified, unconstructed ground of identity. The shentong teachings, however, usually require meditation in order to reveal the actual experience, the actual realization, of this fundamental ground. We cannot reach this ground through our intellect alone. We need to open to it throughout our whole body and being.

One of my favorite descriptions of the shentong view comes from the contemporary Tibetan teacher Khenpo Tsultrim Gyamtso Rinpoche. He claims that although all of the content of our experience is conceptually constructed and can therefore be viewed as not truly existent, the essence of life is unconstructed and therefore does truly exist. He writes, "It is completely free from any conceptualizing process and knows in a way that is completely foreign to the conceptual mind. It is completely unimaginable in fact. That is why it can be said to truly exist."

He also says, "The essence of the non-conceptual Wisdom mind cannot be grasped by the conceptual mind and so, from the point of view of the conceptual mind, it is without essence; from its own point of view it is absolute reality."[7]

Both the rangtong and shentong paths teach that we are not who we think we are and that the world is not what we think it is. But they differ significantly in their view of what we actually are and what the world actually is.

There have been attempts over the centuries to reconcile the two views, to claim that they are really both getting to the same thing.

But, in general, each of the two schools of thought just thinks the other is wrong. They each like to claim that the other is a preparation for getting to their own view. The rangtong adherents think that the teaching of Buddha-nature, or a ground consciousness, is just reassurance for people who are not yet ready to face that there is nothing there. And the shentong adherents feel that the no-ground teaching is for students who are still so identified with their constructed identity that they need to be told it is all an illusion, that there is really nothing there to grasp on to, before they can be open enough to realize the subtle ground of their being.

That said, both views are helpful in pointing out each other's potential pitfalls. There is a danger, in the shentong view, that students will attempt to grasp on to, or to imagine, the pervasive space of fundamental consciousness, instead of opening to it. It can become an object of our awareness, like any other object, rather than realized as our own bare subjectivity. And there is a danger for adherents of the rangtong view that they will remain fixed in an intellectual stance that limits the perceptual immediacy that they seek. They also may never arrive at the actual experience of oneness that arises when we uncover the ground of our being.

In the West, the rangtong teaching of no ground is so much more prevalent than the shentong view that I have heard even many Buddhist teachers refer to it as the only view, as "what Buddhism says." In the psychotherapy field, the dominant understanding of the human psyche has been that it is made of mental constructs and nothing else. We form templates, or schema, based on our earliest experiences, which continue to shape our experience of ourselves and our world for the rest of our lives. With just a few exceptions, contemporary psychotherapists have either denied or ignored the possibility of a unified ground of being beyond these constructs. This common view among psychotherapists meant that as Buddhism became popular in the West, many therapists readily embraced and integrated into their work the rangtong denial of a foundational, unified ground of being.

The popularity of mindfulness forms of meditation and their incorporation into Western psychotherapy modalities, even though they are focused on bodily experience, has in general supported Western psychotherapy's rejection of an essence or ground of being. Mindfulness techniques cultivate the ability to observe even tiny shifts in one's experience. However, the focus of these practices is specifically on the content of experience. With few exceptions, they do not provide instructions for accessing a unified ground of consciousness.

As an example of how fully the Buddhist "empty of itself" philosophy has been accepted in Western psychology, here is a quote from Peter Levine, one of the most influential contemporary psychotherapists:

> Paradoxically, the only way that we can know ourselves is in learning to be mindfully aware of the moment-to-moment goings-on of our body and mind as they exist through various situations occurring in time. We have no experience of anything that is permanent or independent of this. Thus there is no ego or self, just a counterfeit construction. While counterintuitive to most of us, this is common "knowledge" to highly experienced meditators.[8]

However, this is not the knowledge or experience of all highly experienced meditators. Highly experienced meditators have been debating exactly this point for many centuries.

As a teacher of fundamental consciousness, I think that the rangtong view may be better known than the shentong because it is simply easier for many people to do the conceptual deconstructive work of disassembling a table into parts than the fine attunement work of actually experiencing the table as made of the same consciousness as their own being. To know ourselves and our environment as pervaded by fundamental consciousness requires us to thoroughly transform ourselves. It is not only a cognitive procedure but a process of deep inward contact, of subtle, precise attunement to the innermost core of our being. In general, as a culture, we are far more familiar with our cognitive processes than with deepening and refining our contact with ourselves. And in my work as a psychotherapist, I have seen that the suppression of thoughts and feelings, even of the sense of our own existence, is how many of us protected ourselves when we were vulnerable children and that we may utilize this same familiar ability in an attempt to follow the advice, quoted above, that was given to Bahiya.

It is undoubtedly true that life is constantly changing, that everything that occurs does so as a result of something occurring before it and that all things exist in an interrelated web of objects and meanings. It is important and awe-inspiring to understand that we are part of this web of existence, that even our smallest action can have far-reaching repercussions. But for me, this intellectual recognition of our place in the universe is not as liberating as the actual experience of oneness that occurs when we open to the undivided ground of consciousness pervading everywhere. As I will describe later in this book, as fundamental consciousness we can discern even more clearly the changing flux of experience. But the foundation of our being, in my experience, is not just emptiness. It is experienced as a blend of emptiness and presence and some element that defies language and feels like existence itself.

Although my work as a nonduality teacher is aligned with the shentong view, I do not speak of fundamental consciousness as a metaphysical reality. I cannot claim to know what it is. Buddhists often speak of it as the nature of the mind, while many Hindu philosophers have asserted that it is the nature of the universe. Still others claim that we have imagined the universe into being and that therefore the base of the mind and the universe are the same.

In the Realization Process, I teach that fundamental consciousness is an experience, but an experience like no other. We uncover it rather than create it. The Buddhists say that it is "self-knowing." It is not something that we are conscious of as an object; rather it occurs when consciousness becomes conscious of itself. The twentieth-century philosopher Nishitani called it our "primordial subjectivity."[9]

But these are just words until you experience it yourself. That is why I almost never speak or write about fundamental consciousness without including practices for the reader to reach this inner depth within themselves, as I do in this book.

2

Are We or Aren't We?

Buddhist and Hindu philosophies, like all religious precepts, carry great and, for some, unquestionable authority. Their insights and practices are, in my opinion, among the greatest gifts that humans have brought to the world. They have brought happiness, sanity, and wisdom to vast numbers of human beings for centuries. However, like all religious teachings, they are open to a wide range of interpretation. As a psychotherapist and nonduality teacher, I have seen some of these interpretations do harm, both psychologically and spiritually. They can lead us away, rather than toward, nondual realization.

The teaching that seems to cause the most confusion is the teaching that there is no self. It has become fashionable among many spiritual teachers and students today to view the self as fiction. When I question these students, many have not been taught and do not know what is meant by the word *self* that they have accepted as not existing.

I have witnessed dedicated spiritual practitioners actively pretending that they do not exist. They blank out their eyes and flatten their emotional expression. They attempt to separate themselves from their sensations, feelings, and thoughts, either by contriving to observe them from outside of themselves or by suppressing them or by denigrating them as illusory. They may hold a fixed focus on "the present moment" by which they often mean whatever is happening outside of their body in their environment. They may even refer to themselves in the third person as "this one."

All of these tactics create a fragmentation and a tension within one's being that is the opposite of the unconstructed, effortless wholeness and oneness of nondual realization. In psychological terms, the attempt to not exist can cause us to dissociate, to disown major elements of our inner life, such as our emotional responses. It splits our internal responses, such as our thoughts and emotions, from our sensory perception of our environment, creating a false division between our internal and external experience. In this way it limits our experience of our internal wholeness and our oneness of self and other. But in my view, nonduality is the unity of subject and object, of inner and outer experience, not the subjugation of one to the other.

THE MEANING OF SELF

The word *self* can be used to refer to a wide variety of experiences, just as not having a self can point to various experiences. *Self* may refer to a separate soul that goes on after death, either to other realms or to subsequent lives. It may mean self-reflective awareness, a self-observation and mental elaboration on whatever we are experiencing. It may mean the false self that we create to protect ourselves or to help us interact with other people with more confidence. And it may, used interchangeably with the word *ego*, mean selfishness or pridefulness, or ambition.

The nonexistence of the self is taught sometimes as a metaphysical reality and sometimes as a practice. As a practice, the negation of our subjectivity is sometimes taught as a way of emptying the mind of labels and elaboration so that we have a more immediate experience of life. However, this is difficult to achieve without a fixed focus on the world outside of ourselves and careful monitoring and suppression of our responses to what is seen, heard, sensed, and cognized.

Also, and perhaps more importantly, it is possible to cultivate a relatively empty, open mind or perceptual facility without opening the rest of our being, such as our heart, our throat, and our pelvis. These parts of our being are often chronically constricted because of ways that we have protected ourselves, mostly in childhood, against overwhelming circumstances. Because of these buried but haunting memories bound in the tissues of our body, an empty mind is not necessarily an end of suffering. The fear, grief, and anger held within our body still influence our mood, the way we view ourselves, and the way we respond to others.

We need to open not just our mind but our whole body and being in order to recognize and release the roots of our psychological distress. We may experience a wide-open vivid awareness of our surroundings by suppressing reflective thought, but we will not necessarily reach our most fundamental nondual realization. The experience of perception without mental elaboration has been described as "having no head."[1] But it can also be viewed as having just a head, just awareness, without opening to the spiritual foundation of the other aspects of our being, such as our capacities for emotion and physical sensation.

Mental elaboration does dissipate, to some extent, when we experience life not just with our head but with the spiritual depth of our whole being. But when we know ourselves as fundamental consciousness, we can also experience mental elaboration without it interfering with our nondual realization. All of our experience—our thoughts, emotions, physical sensations, and perceptions—move through the stillness of fundamental consciousness that pervades our body and environment as a unity, without changing our realization of that pervasive ground. This includes our reflections on our sensory experience. For example, as fundamental consciousness, we can perceive the sunset clearly, as well as enjoy it and comment on it to ourselves or others. Neither our internal responses nor our mental commentary will obstruct either our sensory experience or our nondual realization. We do not need to limit any aspect of our experience to be whole within our body and one with our surroundings.

Self can also refer to our constructed, or "false," self. The constructed self does need to dissolve to some extent for us to realize fundamental consciousness. We create a false self out of ideas and images based on the roles we play in our lives, such "I am a teacher," our notions about our personality, as in "I am a good person" or "I am a clever person," and our identifications with our culture or psychological history, such as "I am a fragile person." These unconscious, constructed identities may limit our spontaneous authentic responses to our surroundings. They may also limit our inward contact with ourselves and obstruct our openness to fundamental consciousness.

The release of these patterns is an important component of our process of realization. However, in the Realization Process, we do not release into empty space, into nothingness. We let go of our constructed identity into fundamental consciousness.

As fundamental consciousness, we do not disappear. Just the opposite. We come, increasingly, to a sense of truly being ourselves. As the false self dissolves, we uncover our ability to see and hear with our own eyes and ears, to really feel whatever we are touching. We uncover the ring of truth in our own voice. We have direct access to whatever we are knowing and feeling in each moment. We may still identify with our social and historical background and with the roles that we serve in the world. We may still feel a particular kinship with communities of people who have similar preferences to our own or who have suffered similar injuries and trauma. But we also know ourselves beyond these identifications, so they do not have the power to grip us in static patterns of embodiment or behavior.

THE EGO

The word *self* is also often used interchangeably with the word *ego*, which also has numerous meanings. When spiritual students speak of attempting to annihilate the ego, they are often referring to conceit or ambition or desire, to acting out of some sort of self-serving agenda. There is often a punitive tone to this endeavor. I have heard teachers proclaim how sneaky the ego is, how we can fool ourselves into believing that we have rid ourselves of it, when it is still lurking there, ready to interfere with our spiritual state and tainting our goodness. I have heard spiritual students react to some mildly self-referential action with "Damn, that's my ego again" as harshly as if they were beating themselves with a stick. This vigilant, self-punitive attitude means that we become a monitor of our thoughts and behavior in a way that creates a schism within ourselves and interferes with our realization of nonduality.

Self-punishment, self-denial, and self-sacrifice have long been a part of many religious practices, but in my view, they have no part to play in nondual realization. We are not attempting to please or appease a judgmental image of God. Nondual realization is primarily for our own enjoyment, our own openness to life, and the depth and authenticity of our own responses to life. Although nondual realization does not require obedience to moral commandments, with this deepening and opening of our own being, there is often a natural emergence of our ability to empathize and the desire to help others.

As the false or egoic self, we may hold rigid ideas or bodily stances of exaggerated self-importance, such as chronic, static postures of inflation or dominance. We may also hold and unconsciously act out of chronic attitudes of shame and submission. But these patterns need to be approached with tenderness and understanding. Their initial causes, usually as ways of navigating our early circumstances, need to be recognized and resolved. We can recognize, resolve, and release these patterns in a way that is healing rather than punitive.

In the process of releasing these rigidly held patterns from our body and mind, we increase our inward contact with ourselves. This produces a natural, uncontrived sense of self-possession. We know ourselves. We can actually experience the feel of our love, our intelligence, and our truth, and this produces a genuine sense of self-esteem. We also gain more access to our true ambition and desires and a better ability to realize our aspirations, as we uncover the authentic ground of our being. Self-esteem, self-motivation, and desire can twist and morph into conceit, greed, and excessive appetite. But this happens when they are thwarted, and when the psychological wounding that produced this twist is not addressed.

All of our human capacities, including our will and agency, our ability to know what we want and aim toward it, are refined and enhanced as we realize fundamental consciousness. This gaining of greater access to our will and agency is important to emphasize. Because it is exactly this ability for knowing our desires and then making decisions and acting to fulfill them that we often lose in traumatic situations. When we are overpowered by a dominant adult or a bullying sibling or peer, we lose access to our own power, our own will. Spiritual teachings that suggest that we have no will of our own, that we are somehow propelled by something other than ourselves, whether it be God or the ground of being, exacerbate our trauma-based relinquishment of our own agency. We do become more spontaneous in our responses to life as we know ourselves as fundamental consciousness. We let go of calculation and our manipulation of ourselves and others, but this should not be confused with a surrendering of our own agency. Even in states of flow, when we are entirely absorbed in what we are doing, the doer has not disappeared. The doer and the doing have become one.

THE PERSONAL GROUND

The no-ground teachings seek to free us from our identification with impermanent aspects of self-experience, such as our sensations, emotions, and thoughts, and then conclude that there is nothing left to experience beyond this flux. But just as misleading, in my view, are those teachings that recognize a ground of consciousness but consider the ground to be impersonal. The word *impersonal* is also subject to interpretation. It can mean universal, something to which we all have potential access, as we all have access to fundamental consciousness. The realization of fundamental consciousness is the same, or a very similar, experience for all of us. But to say that the ground of our being is impersonal can also imply that it is something that eradicates or transcends our sense of our own personal existence. And this is not true. When we know ourselves as fundamental consciousness, we have reached our deepest roots inward; we are situated within the innermost core of our own personal being.

Advaita Vedanta teaches that the whole universe is made of consciousness. This consciousness is impersonal, being everywhere the same. According to this teaching the impersonal consciousness pervades the shape of the various objects we find in the world, but it is still the same one consciousness, just as the clay that makes up a pot and a vase are the same substance in different forms.

This is a compelling and beautiful idea. But as a realization, fundamental consciousness is not experienced as impersonal. For unlike a clay pot or vase, a human being has the capacity to realize their basic identity, to uncover the basic stuff of which they are made. We do not submerge our identity in the pervasive space of fundamental consciousness. Rather we uncover this foundation of ourselves as our true identity. For each of us, fundamental consciousness feels like who we are. This is not only a concept but an experience. We have, as the embodiment of fundamental consciousness, a palpable sense of our own existence. There is a sense of being actually oneself, of uncovering a deeply, invisibly rooted, authentic identity.

This means that our realization of fundamental consciousness brings us into the root of our own personal existence at the same time as it enters us into an experience that is potentially shared with all other human beings. We mature as individuals at the same time as we mature in our experience of oneness with our surroundings. We know ourselves as individual and universal at the same time. In reaching the most personal core of our own being, we find our oneness with all other beings.

A point of clarification: to know our own identity as fundamental consciousness pervading our own body and all of the objects that we perceive in our environment does not mean that we feel that we are those objects in our environment. The realization of fundamental consciousness does not eradicate the difference between self and other. Rather, it clearly reflects and reveals the distinction between our own being and our surroundings while at the same time revealing our underlying unity with everyone and everything that we encounter.

As fundamental consciousness, we have the choice in any moment to experience ourselves as separate, as having permeable edges, or to experience ourselves as clear through space without boundaries. But even as clear through space, our locus is still within our body. We live in our own receptive, responsive center of the pervasive expanse of fundamental consciousness. We never mistake ourselves for the lamp or the table or other people.

FINDING THE SELF

The rangtong Buddhist teachings often point out that when we try to find ourselves, we cannot. We only find passing fragments of experience and those separate building blocks of experience such as emotions, thoughts, and sensations. But this instruction—to try (and fail) to find ourselves—also begs the question, Who is looking? When we watch ourselves, we make an object of ourselves; we become another labeled object, another conceptual phantom. But who is watching? That, to me, is the mystery. If there is someone watching, then someone must be there.

We can only theorize or imagine that we do not exist. We can never experience that we do not exist, because who would be experiencing it? That "who" exists. We can speculate that beyond experience there is nonexistence, but that can only be speculation.

Shankara wrote, "To refute the Self is impossible, for he who tries to refute it is the Self."[2] The ninth-century Zen master Rinzai expressed it like this: "Who then can understand the Dharma[3] and can listen to it? The one here before your very eyes, brilliantly clear and shining without any form—there he is who can understand the Dharma you are listening to. If you can really grasp this, you are not different from the Buddhas and patriarchs. Ceaselessly he is right here, conspicuously present."[4]

Rinzai also said, "Followers of the Way: he who is now listening to the Dharma, he is not the four elements; he is the one who can use the four elements" and "If you want to get free from birth and death . . . know and take hold of the one who is now listening to the Dharma."[5]

This teaching states explicitly that there is someone there and that someone is not an object but a subject, the one who can listen and teach. Even though we cannot find a self as an object, it is still there, listening, responding. So the one who is reading these words right now (you) is the one who becomes more apparent, more accessible, as they know themselves as fundamental consciousness.

This is an understanding of self as conceptually ungraspable, as a primary dimension of subjectivity that does not construct fixed representations of itself. We can say that this primary dimension is impersonal in the sense that it is experienced in apparently the same way by anyone who uncovers it. Yet, as the most fundamental experience that we can each have of ourselves, it is deeply, quintessentially personal.

But what of the changing content of our experience? What of the preferences, talents, desires, and memories that make us all different from each other? Are they eradicated by the realization of this universal dimension of experience?

As we realize ourselves as fundamental consciousness, we gradually let go of the rigid protective organizations of mind and body and the fixed mental attitudes and concepts of ourselves that obscure our basic nature. But this awakening does not eradicate our personality. It does not erase our unique characteristics, such as the sound of our voice, our particular sense of humor, or the familial and cultural history that has helped shape us with its specific tastes and values, gestures and expressions. As fundamental consciousness, we can recognize our individual preferences, desires, and aptitudes even more clearly. Our unique personality sheds its constraints and becomes even more freely and spontaneously expressed. As Nishitani wrote, "It is the field in which each and every thing—as an absolute center, possessed of an absolutely unique individuality—becomes manifest as it is in itself."[6]

And this realization of fundamental consciousness does not diminish our ability to remember our past or to reflect on our present experience or to relate with other human beings. If it did, it would mean that our nondual realization was momentary, a quick dart into the absolute and then an inevitable return to "conventional" reality in which we cannot help but remember, reflect, and relate to others. But realization is not momentary; it matures into an ongoing experience of our fundamental nature. We can sustain this realization because the content of our experience is encompassed and clearly revealed by the primary dimension of our being.

We have an accessible, ongoing experience of an undivided ground of being that enables us to think, feel, sense, and act at the same time, as an undivided whole. We have agency, desire, and preferences, we have talents and weaknesses, and we have continuity over time, the ability to look back with memory and forward with aspiration, seeing ourselves as basically the same person in both directions. We each have the integrative ability to connect the information coming in from our senses with our learned knowledge of the world. We have edges—even though we extend beyond our body energetically, our skin envelopes and contains us. It does not matter whether or not we call these experiences "self." But it does matter if we feel that we need to sacrifice any of these important characteristics of our human experience to realize our spiritual potential.

Why are so many spiritual students willing to sacrifice themselves on the pyre of nonexistence? This is a question that often arises for me when I see people regarding with contempt the telltale signs of their own aliveness in the name of nonduality: when I see a friend, who I know to be a lively, vital woman, now doing a convincing imitation of an empty-eyed zombie; when a new student refers to herself by name, as if the name belongs to some separate and lesser human that she must cart around with her; when a woman refers to her thoughts and desires as something "the mind" is doing or wanting, as if her mind were some entity separate from herself; when I see a man who is already afraid to feel emotions tighten his chest even tighter than his usual chronic tension because he believes that enlightenment is a state without feeling.

One reason for this determined suppression of themselves is that they have learned from their respected teachers or books that this is the path to liberation from suffering, to spiritual elevation. Throughout history, people have wanted to be closer to God, to goodness. We want to be cleansed of what we believe to be our bad thoughts and acts, and we are often willing to do pretty much anything to accomplish this and to believe anyone who assures us they can bring us there.

My work as a psychotherapist has shown me other reasons as well. Almost all human beings grow up with some amount of self-loathing. Based on our parents' anger and disappointment in us, no matter how rare an occurrence, together with our own disappointment in ourselves—the ways that we do not measure up to our own or others' standards of goodness, intelligence, beauty, and accomplishment—and the rejections from friends and lovers over the years that can cause us to lose self-esteem, self-worth, and self-trust, this self-loathing is one of the biggest obstacles not only to our sense of well-being but to our process of psychological healing. It may cause us to feel relieved at the idea that we can simply erase ourselves.

Also, many of us are already skilled at diminishing ourselves, at constricting those parts of ourselves, especially when we are children, that are not met with safety and acceptance. We hold back our tears by constricting the anatomy involved in crying. We tighten our sexual organs against violation. We limit our emotions, our intelligence, our voice, and our power and vitality to mirror or accommodate or protect ourselves against the important adults in our early lives.

So when a spiritual teacher tells us that enlightened people do not feel emotion or that our opinions are just the misbehavior of our ego, we are both ready and able to adjust ourselves to that teacher's requirements.

I do not mean to dismiss the teaching of nonexistence itself, which has its uses as a spiritual practice, but only this literal interpretation of it, only the use of it to constrain the very life that nondual realization can set free. When we let go of our grip on ourselves, we come more fully into existence. This is not some impersonal theoretical existence but the innermost depth of our own actual, personal being. As we realize the fundamental ground of ourselves, it is our own love that blooms in our hearts. Our own impulse that moves us to speak or act. Our own creativity that moves the paint on the canvas, the words on the page. To attempt to distance ourselves from the innermost core of our own humanness also obstructs our entranceway into fundamental consciousness. What may be one single light, one universal undivided consciousness, is for each of us our own light, pervading our body and our world.

3

Our Birthright

One of the most important things to understand about nondual realization is that it is possible. Not as only a peak experience but as an ongoing transformation of our being.

Many Buddhist and Hindu teachers describe the enlightened state in the first person. I have already quoted Shankara claiming "I am the supreme Brahman" and Longchenpa seemingly joyfully sharing, "I Longchen Rabjam . . . experience everything as embraced within a blissful expanse, a single nondual expanse." Although there is no way for me to know their true motivation so many centuries ago, I assume that their intent was not to brag about the rarity and superiority of their realization but to invite others to access this same realization themselves.

Yet I have found that among many contemporary spiritual students, the description of the realization of all-pervasive consciousness in the spiritual literature is often regarded with reverence and awe, as a mysterious, semi-mythical achievement, available only to spiritual giants. They consider it to be too far out to be of practical use to ordinary people.

I cannot know if I am experiencing and teaching exactly what Longchenpa did. But judging from his many careful descriptions of his experience, it is certainly similar. However, the realization of the vast "blissful expanse" that Longchenpa and many other Hindu and Buddhist teachers point to and that I am describing in this book is a relative experience, a matter of degree.

There is a definite and extraordinary shift that occurs when we realize fundamental consciousness pervading our own body and everything around us as a continuous expanse of luminous space. All of the objects and living forms that we encounter appear to be pervaded by or made of consciousness—the same undivided expanse of consciousness that pervades our own body. But once that shift into oneness has occurred, we can continue to realize fundamental consciousness by continuing to open to that pervasive space throughout more of our body. So it is certainly likely that Longchenpa and other revered teachers who wrote about fundamental consciousness were far more realized than I am. But I do feel confident that it is the same realization, even if it is to a lesser degree.

A Buddhist text, the *Tathagatagarbha Sutra*,[1] describes the Buddha saying to his students, "When I regard all beings with my Buddha eye, I see that hidden within their negative mental traits there is seated augustly and unmovingly the Buddha's wisdom, the Buddha's vision, and the Buddha's body."

There is much debate among Buddhist scholars about the interpretation of this sutra, and again, I cannot know with certainty what the writer of this passage meant. But my understanding is that the Buddha is saying that he can see, with the sensitivity of his innate Buddha-nature, that the people listening to him also have the same nature, along with its potential wisdom, vision, and body. Someone who has realized the essential nature of his own being is assuring his listeners that everyone has within them the same essential nature that he has realized within himself. I understand it to be an invitation to find this primary nature within ourselves.

I cannot claim to the reader who is setting out to explore this potential that you will gain extraordinary powers. But I can predict a deepening and refinement of all your human capacities. And just as the Buddha says in the *Tathagatagarbha Sutra*, it will be a transformation of every facet of your being—including your experience of embodiment, your understanding, your emotional capacity, and your perception.

Based on my many years of experience as a nonduality teacher, I can claim that the degree of realization that I have achieved and that

I describe in the following chapters is available to everyone. You can uncover your fundamental nature as a single expanse of consciousness embracing and pervading all of the changing content of your experience. This realization is your birthright. It is your own self-nature. You have innately within you, seated "augustly and unmoving," the Buddha's body, wisdom, compassion, and perception. It is your own body, your own being, unveiled.

Part 2

THE PATH

4

The Realization Process

In the Realization Process, nondual realization is the uncovering of a fundamental, undivided dimension of consciousness. We experience unity, an unbroken continuity, within our own body and between our internal and external experience. This is an unbroken transparency, or permeability, of ourselves and everything and everyone around us.

Fundamental consciousness is experienced (it experiences itself) as stillness—undivided stillness that coincides with all of the movement of life within our body and within our environment in each moment. It is separate from the content of our experience and at the same time everywhere within it. It is disentangled from the movement of life, allowing that movement to flow without obstruction.

This means that, as fundamental consciousness, we let go of our grip on ourselves and our environment. We allow ourselves to experience the clarity of our thoughts and the full impact of our emotions, physical sensations, and perceptions. This is freedom; freedom from our own constricting grasp on our body and being.

In the Buddhist and Hindu spiritual literature, the ground of our being is described as "uncreated," "self-existing," and "self-originating." We do not imagine or construct it. We open to it. We uncover it. As fundamental consciousness, we feel as if we have stripped away constructed experience and found the unmodified consciousness beyond any construction. That is why fundamental consciousness can be described as essence, as what is already there beyond or more subtle than our constructed, learned experience of how we perceive and know ourselves and our world. This does not necessarily mean that we each have an individual essence, or an immutable soul. But it does mean that we can each uncover a sense of authenticity, of truly existing, that is simultaneously separate—contained within our own form—and fundamentally unified with other people and everything in our environment.

Most Asian spiritual teachings that describe a spiritual ground state clearly that this ground is both immanent and transcendent. Advaita Vedanta, for example, says that atman, the true self, is identical to Brahman, the all-pervasive consciousness. "The man of knowledge realizes that Atman, or the inmost soul of the individual, which is vividly felt in the heart and which sustains the body, the senses and the mind, is one with Brahman, which sustains the universe."[1]

As a contemporary nondual path, the Realization Process elaborates on the lived transformation that occurs in each of us as we uncover this immanent and transcendent ground. It addresses the personal and relational richness and depth that nondual realization brings to life on earth.

The Realization Process specifically addresses how nondual realization affects our experience of our body. But not just the physical body or even the subtle energy body. I mean the body that we experience as made of fundamental consciousness. As the body of fundamental consciousness, we experience ourselves as separate and whole and at the same time unified with our surroundings. To realize fundamental consciousness with our whole body means that we are conscious and in contact with ourselves throughout our whole body and being. This deepened inward contact reveals innate (unconstructed) qualities of our humanness, the felt qualities of our aliveness. It also deepens and enhances our contact with other people and with all of nature.

THE METHOD

In the Realization Process we open to the unity and transparency of nondual realization by inhabiting the internal space of our body. Wherever we inhabit our body, we are both in contact with ourselves and open to our surroundings. For example, if we inhabit the internal depth of our chest, we are both in contact with ourselves in our chest and open and emotionally responsive to our environment. We experience the present moment occurring within and outside of our body at the same time.

However, the realization of fundamental consciousness is not just openness, not just contact with ourselves and responsiveness to our surroundings. To reach the most subtle dimension of ourselves, we need to inhabit our body, and we also need to access a subtle channel that runs through the vertical core of our torso, neck, and head. This channel has been called sushumna in yoga and the central channel in Tibetan Buddhism. When we reach this innermost vertical core of our being, we realize that we *are* fundamental consciousness, that it is not something separate from us. We need to contact ourselves more deeply even than a feeling or perception of emptiness to reach the ground consciousness that is experienced as our primary nature. This means that when people experience the ground or essence of their being as impersonal, they have not gone deeply enough or with a subtle enough focus into the innermost core of their body.

Some nondual teachings claim that we do not need to do any sort of practice to realize nonduality. If this is our true nature and if that nondual aspect of ourselves is already there within us, they reason, then we just need to let go and relax into it. Although relaxation is always a positive shift from a gripping, anxious state, most people will not land in fundamental consciousness if they just relax. When instructed to "just let go" of themselves, people will often let go from the surface of their body, into the space around them. They will feel better, and they may feel more alert, but they will not experience their own being as subtle pervasive fundamental consciousness. Also, in this "no practice" approach, it is necessary to keep remembering to "just relax." This can be particularly challenging during times of stress or discomfort, times when the realization of fundamental consciousness would be particularly helpful.

In the Realization Process, we practice inhabiting the internal space of our body and the subtle vertical channel of our body to let go of our habitual grip on ourselves from within our whole body and from within the core of our being. As we are gradually able to let go in this way, we lay bare our basic nature as a lasting transformation, not as something that we have to remember to evoke.

Nondual realization, as it is understood and uncovered in the Realization Process, is not a peak experience or an understanding or a behavioral shift. It is an ongoing transformation of our being that, once realized, does not require any volitional action to maintain.

Although the Realization Process is aligned with those teachings that recognize our potential to uncover a fundamental, unified ground of being, it also differs from many traditional teachings in important ways. In the Realization Process, nondual realization is recognized as the basis of personal as well as spiritual maturity. As we uncover fundamental consciousness pervading our whole body, we experience the deepening of all of our human capacities, including our capacity for connection with other people. This process often uncovers areas of limitation in our body and in our beliefs that require our attention and healing. In this way psychological healing becomes an integrated aspect of nondual awakening.

In the next chapters, I will describe how nondual realization gradually develops our experience of wholeness, depth, steadiness, fluidity, permeability, and connection and how each of these aspects of fundamental consciousness contributes to our effectiveness as human beings and our enjoyment of our lives.

I include the main practices of the Realization Process for realizing our own nature as fundamental consciousness. The practices of the Realization Process are not the realization of nonduality itself. They are volitional attunements designed to evoke the self-arising of nondual realization. They can give us an immediate attunement to fundamental consciousness that facilitates the gradual, spontaneous, effortless awakening to our fundamental nature. Although we may have peak experiences of the oneness of all-pervasive consciousness, a stable realization rarely occurs without consistent practice. We need to refine and deepen our inward contact with our body in order to open to this subtle ground of our being and experience it as our primary nature.

HOW TO PRACTICE THE REALIZATION PROCESS

The practices of the Realization Process are gentle, and the experience that they are designed to evoke emerges gradually. You can use the instructions provided in this book as an introduction to the work. If you find the practices useful, there are many others that you can learn from a Realization Process teacher. There are also Realization Process workshops and classes offered throughout the world and online, if you would like the support of a community of practitioners.

To practice on your own, you can record yourself reading the instructions and follow them at your own pace. With these practices, you become your own teacher, your own guide to your own being. Please be a gentle, patient teacher. Although, at the beginning of our path, we may have sudden and dramatic but temporary glimpses of oneness, the actual realization of oneness is a gradual shift that affects our whole being. We can help it along, but it is a natural process, like a ripening, and it takes its own time.

It is more effective to do a little consistent practice—for example ten to thirty minutes at a time—than to do long stretches of practice only once in a while. It is also best to do the practice methodically and then let it go and not try to hold on to the experience that you had during your practice period. After each practice, sit for a moment, inhabiting your whole body and attuning to the space of fundamental consciousness pervading you and your environment. Let yourself experience whatever the practice has evoked. And then, let go of it. Go about your day. With consistent practice, you will gradually find yourself living within your whole body and knowing yourself as the pervasive space of fundamental consciousness all the time, without effort.

Traditionally, the realization of oneself as fundamental consciousness has been considered an advanced stage of spiritual attainment. But I have found in teaching the Realization Process that anyone who feels drawn to it and is willing to do the steady practice of inward attunement is capable of this realization.

Many spiritual traditions claim that you need a teacher to transmit their own realization of fundamental consciousness to you. Some degree of transmission occurs whenever two or more people spend time together. But for a lasting transformation to occur, we need to let go of our own grip on ourselves from within. No one can do that for us. Realization Process teachers do not teach by transmitting their realization to their students. We offer practices that people can use to awaken themselves.

Fundamental consciousness is your own nature; it is accessible within your own body. You do not need to receive it from someone else. Nor do you need permission from anyone to find this deeper, subtler contact with yourself. And you do not need anyone to tell you that you are now ready to pursue this advanced stage of spiritual experience. If you want to do it, you can.

You also do not need anyone to affirm your realization. This is not a test to pass, not a status to achieve in the eyes of anyone else. The emergence of fundamental consciousness in your body and your surroundings is unmistakable. It is experienced as luminous stillness pervading everywhere. Your own body and everything around you appear to be made of a single unified, unmoving expanse of space. There is no other confirmation of your realization beyond the profound openness, radiance, and authenticity of fundamental consciousness.

Only keep in mind that fundamental consciousness is absolutely still. It is even more subtle than the vibrating, pulsing energetic dimension of life. It is even more subtle than physical air. We experience it pervading the physical air. But we cannot reach this stillness by holding still. We uncover the stillness through inward attunement to ourselves.

Also, fundamental consciousness pervades your own body at the same time as it pervades your surroundings—it is not an outward projection or inflation of yourself. Fundamental consciousness, pervading you and everything and everyone around you, provides you with a sense of equality between your own being and all others. Everything appears to be made of the same subtle ground.

With the realization of fundamental consciousness, you become more whole, more authentic, loving, and aware as you contact yourself more deeply within your own being. Sometimes people feel fear of the unknown, of letting go of their protective grip on themselves, of shedding their constructed identity. They may ask, "Who will I be if I realize fundamental consciousness?" But this question is answered by the experience itself. This is especially true of the approach offered in this book in which nondual realization is based on inward contact with your body. As you realize nonduality, you do not dissolve into nothingness. You settle ever more fully into the familiar shape and feel of your own body and being.

As you focus more deeply inward, it is possible that you may uncover painful memories or release painful emotions that have been bound within your body since childhood. Some of these constrictions may release easily, without your even having an awareness of a memory or emotion. Or you may feel momentarily sad or angry or afraid.

However, our deeply held constrictions, which are usually related to ways that we needed to protect ourselves against severe or repetitive or very early trauma, may not release this easily. The Realization Process has a release technique for letting go of these constrictions, along with resolving the painful memories associated with them. For more about that aspect of the Realization Process, please read *Trauma and the Unbound Body*[2] or contact a senior Realization Process teacher (see the Realization Process website, realizationprocess.org, for a list of instructors).

It is not necessary for us to release all of the psychologically based constrictions from our body in order to realize fundamental consciousness. But the constrictions do obstruct our ability to fully inhabit our body. The more we release the constrictions, the more fully we can inhabit our body and the more fully we can open to fundamental consciousness.

If painful memories and emotions occur as you inhabit your body, or if you feel that there is so much constriction in your body that you cannot begin to inhabit it, it is best to include psychological healing with your spiritual practice, in the company of a skilled, compassionate listener and guide.

Sometimes people experience emotional responses to the process of realization itself. The most common emotion is relief. It is not unusual for people to find themselves crying with the relief of coming home to themselves, of fitting within their body and knowing themselves as whole but also as deeply connected with everything around them. Or we may shed tears at the exquisite beauty of a world pervaded by luminous space. There may be regret for the years that we have lived without this experience, but that is usually quickly supplanted by the joy of finally being there.

5

Wholeness

Every being is changed to a perfectly coherent radiance made
transparent through the illumination of the transcendent.

—Kukai

One of the most noticeable changes that occur when we realize fundamental consciousness is that we experience ourselves as whole. One might think that self-other oneness is an unbounded state, and in a sense, it is. Fundamental consciousness is experienced as space. And yet, when we uncover fundamental consciousness pervading our whole body and environment, an internal coherence occurs within our body, within our individual being, that we experience as internal wholeness. We know ourselves as a whole at the same time as we experience ourselves as clear-through openness to the space that pervades our body and environment.

As fundamental consciousness, our internal wholeness is distinct and yet inseparable from our self-other oneness. We cannot and do not experience one without the other. When we uncover fundamental consciousness as the ground of our individual being, we uncover our self-other oneness at the same time. However, this is not a displacing or merging of one arena of experience with another. Fundamental consciousness pervades and therefore clearly reveals the delineation of our own internal being from our external surroundings.

Rather than erasing our individuality, this ground pervading our own body produces a felt sense of our separate individual being. We know our edges, even though those edges are made of empty space. We know ourselves as a separate transparency within the transparency that is everywhere. We know ourselves as an individual light within the one light that is everywhere. When we move, transparency moves through transparency, light moves through light.

Our internal wholeness is made of fundamental consciousness. We experience that we are conscious everywhere in our body simultaneously. This consciousness is contact. We are in contact with our whole being at once. We have a felt sense of being—of living—everywhere in our body. We experience ourselves as possessing internal volume, of being space and taking up space.

This is a tangible experience. It is a shift from knowing ourselves abstractly, from having an idea about who we are that may change in different circumstances, to experiencing ourselves as an unchanging, nonconceptual ground of consciousness.

To be conscious everywhere in our body is mind-body integration. Or it might better be described as being-body integration. Most of us are not integrated in this way. We are not situated, not present, within the internal space of our body. We may live in front of or above our body. We may be present as just a fraction of ourselves within our body. And we may experience ourselves as present in only a part of our body, such as our head or our chest, which may change in different situations.

The main reason for this division between our being and our body is the protective and compensatory pattern of constrictions that we all hold to some extent within our body. We create these patterns of constriction, mainly in childhood and adolescence, to limit the impact of abrasive or traumatic events in our lives or to hold back the expression of emotions, words, or behaviors that might not be met with love and approval from our family and peers, such as tears or anger. For example, we cannot stop ourselves from crying without tensing those parts of our anatomy that are involved in crying. We cannot protect ourselves from hearing abrasive sounds, such as angry voices, or block unpleasant odors, such as the smell of smoke or whiskey on our parents' breath, without clamping down on the anatomy involved in those sensory experiences. We may also mirror and retain our parents' patterns of constriction. If these constrictions are repeated over time, they become rigid, unconscious limitations in our body and being that obstruct and fragment our contact with the internal space of our body. We cannot contact, we cannot inhabit, those areas of our body that we have constricted.

We also live outside of our body because we may have learned to relate to other people in that way, by coming forward toward them, by projecting ourselves, our energy, outward toward the other person. This may even be intensified in our increasingly digital world, where we attempt to connect with each other through the screens of our digital devices. Although we may feel that this outward projection brings us closer to the other person, this pattern of leaving our own body to make contact actually diminishes our ability to truly connect with them. Our capacity for genuine contact and our ability to respond with love, understanding, and pleasure, as well as to see, hear, and touch another person is based on our degree of internal contact with our own body.

We may also have developed a pattern of coming forward toward whatever we are focused on in order to concentrate better. Or we may live in a habitual pattern of outward vigilance to our surroundings, to be on guard for any threat. To actually live within one's body is a new experience for most people, and it often feels like a great relief. To live outside of the body requires tension, even if it is chronic, unconscious tension. To inhabit the body is to be at ease within our own skin.

Our energy field does extend beyond our body when we live within our body. However, the internal coherence that occurs when we realize fundamental consciousness is contained within our skin. As fundamental consciousness, we know ourselves throughout our whole body, including our skin. We also experience a sense of ownership when we live within our body. Our arms feel like our own arms, for example. Our body feels like our own body.

You can try this out for yourself. Take a moment to inhabit your arms and hands, to feel present within them. Now let yourself experience that these are your arms, your hands. This may help you experience the internal coherence that I am describing.

To inhabit our body is very different from being aware of our body. When we are aware of our body, we observe our thoughts, emotions, and physical sensations from outside of ourselves. When we live within our body, we observe our experience from within. As if, for example, our feet could know themselves from within themselves. If our hands are cold, it feels as if our hands themselves are conscious of the sensation of coldness.

As the undivided ground of fundamental consciousness, we have access to our whole being all at once. We do not have to feel our hands and then our feet, for example, or one hand and then the other. We can feel, from the inside, our whole body at the same time. If we move even one part of our body, even one hand or one finger, our whole body and whole being are engaged in the movement.

We also have access to all of our human capacities at once. Our capacities for cognition, emotion, physical sensation, and perception function in unison. This means that we can think and feel and sense and perceive at the same time. We are unified within our own body, and our internal experience is unified, or continuous with, our experience of our surroundings.

Although we still have the capacity to narrow our focus on one aspect of our experience, all of our activities engage our whole being. We can write, for example, with both mental clarity and emotion, with the freedom of our authentic voice, while being open to the spontaneous flow of our creativity, while moving our hands on the keyboard, while hearing the sounds of the birds outside and seeing in our periphery the field and the trees beyond our window. All of these elements flow through the undivided expanse of fundamental consciousness that pervades our body and environment as a unity.

To receive and respond to life with our whole being enriches and expands every aspect of our experience. In the Realization Process, we do most of the practices with our eyes closed at first and then with our eyes open. This is partly so that we can take our realization out into our daily lives, with our eyes open. But it is also because our senses have been established in accord with how we live in our body.

They mirror the patterns of fragmentation and constriction within our whole body. For example, if we live more in the top of our body than the bottom, we will look out mostly through the top of our eyes. I do not mean that we will focus upward but that we are looking more through the top portion of our eyes than through the bottom of our eyes. If we live just in our midbody, we will see through a narrow band in the middle of our eyes, and if we live mostly in our lower body, we will see through the lower portion of our eyes. This means that where we are situated in ourselves changes how our environment appears to us.

Here is a short attunement to illustrate this:

> Choose an object in your environment that has a lot of texture, such as a carpet or the drapes, or a sweater. Observing yourself carefully, let yourself see the texture of the object. You will probably find that you need to shift downward within your body to see the texture of the object.

When we inhabit our whole body, we look out of our whole eyes, we hear with the whole breadth of our hearing, we touch, smell, and taste with our whole being. Experiencing life from within our whole body also increases the intensity and depth of our experience. Our emotions flow more deeply through us. All of the sensory world—sounds, sights, smells, tastes, and textures—register more clearly, more vividly.

However, to inhabit our whole body also provides a container of tolerance for that depth and intensity. We are both impacted more deeply and more resilient. We can encompass whatever happens to us not by diminishing our emotional responses to it but by remaining present to those emotions with our whole being. We will still suffer grief or anger or fear, but those emotions, no matter how powerful, will be tempered by our understanding and grounded and supported by our experience of physical sensation. This whole-body resilience can also help us tolerate the intense emotions that we may need to feel as we release them in order to heal from the effects of trauma. It can also help highly sensitive people to live more comfortably, to cushion the impact of abrasive stimuli that might otherwise be overwhelming.

The internal coherence that occurs as we realize fundamental consciousness contributes in many ways to our psychological health and maturity. It is as important for us to be able to feel separate and in contact with our own thoughts, emotions, and sensations as it is for us to feel open and in contact with the world around us.

Even our spiritual maturity, our realization of our self-other oneness, depends on our contact with our separateness. As you will see in the next chapter, we open to fundamental consciousness by first inhabiting the internal space of the body. We do this because fundamental consciousness is a dimension of unity. It pervades both our body and our environment at the same time. If we do not experience it pervading our body, it is not yet fundamental consciousness and not yet oneness. So separateness and oneness are both essential to the nature of nondual realization. We mature as whole, distinct individuals at the same time as we transcend our individuality.

6

Attunement to Fundamental Consciousness

In the following practice, you attune directly to fundamental consciousness pervading your body and environment. The practice provides several entranceways into this subtle experience. The main entranceway is through inhabiting the internal space of your body so that you can open to fundamental consciousness throughout your whole body.

Another entranceway into fundamental consciousness in this practice is through balancing awareness of various points in the body, such as the space inside your knees, hip sockets, and shoulder sockets. This same balancing of matching points in the body can be done anywhere in the body, such as the centers of both palms or the right and left hinges of the jaw. If you are missing part of your body that is mentioned in the following instructions, you may still be able to experience this subtle balanced awareness, but you can also skip that particular instruction if it is uncomfortable for you to focus in that area.

Balancing your awareness of matching points in the body can help you enter into the stillness of fundamental consciousness. Fundamental consciousness is experienced as stillness because it is the dimension of perfect balance. It is important not to attempt to experience this stillness by holding still. The stillness emerges as we attune to it, and, with practice, as we let go into it, as we experience it as the ground of our own being.

Everything else in life moves—our emotions, thoughts, sensations, perceptions, and even our circumstances. All of the life around us and within us is in constant movement, constant change. The more we know ourselves as the stillness of fundamental consciousness, the more freely, deeply, and fluidly all of the movement of life flows through us. So stillness and fluidity are simultaneous in our nondual experience. That is why, in this practice, you attune to the stillness of fundamental consciousness and the movement of your breath at the same time. It is a preparation for being able to stabilize your realization of fundamental consciousness by experiencing the stillness of the ground and the movement of life at the same time.

In the Realization Process we make a distinction between the ground—fundamental consciousness—and the content of experience. However, we are not separate from the content of our experience in a detached way. Rather, we are disentangled from the movement of life so that we can allow it to flow and change. To be disentangled from the content of experience means not to latch on to it in an effort to somehow capture it or keep it from changing and not to clamp down on it to limit its impact.

Another entranceway into fundamental consciousness in this practice is attuning to the quality of self. By "quality of self" I mean a particular quality that feels like "self." It is the same or a very similar quality in all of us in the same way that the feeling of love is the same in all of us or similar enough for us to recognize when someone is feeling or expressing it. We cannot put into words what this quality is—just as we cannot truly convey in words what love feels like.

I have included the instruction to attune to the quality of self in this practice because, interestingly, attuning to this quality enters us into the whole internal space of our body and in this way facilitates our entranceway into the pervasive space of fundamental consciousness. I do not mean to point to a conceptual, ontological, or metaphysical notion of a self but rather an experience that we all have the potential to access. It is not your own sense of self but just a quality, a feeling, that helps us uncover the pervasive space of fundamental consciousness. It feels similar to the quality of "I am." If you cannot feel the quality of self, you can skip this instruction or try to experience the quality of "I am."

All of the qualities that we attune to in the body in this practice can help us open to the spontaneous emerging of fundamental consciousness. Realizing fundamental consciousness unveils these authentic qualities that are innate within our body. Because these qualities are innate—not constructed or imagined—they are integral to the fundamental ground of our being. I have ascribed labels to these qualities, such as gender, power, love, voice, and understanding, in order to help people attune to them. However, if these words do not fit with your own experience, the labels themselves are not important. You can label them in any way that describes your own experience of the qualities of your being within your body.

Note: If you are very diffuse energetically—if you feel empty inside your body and vulnerable and "spaced out" a lot of the time, you should just practice the first part of the exercise—inhabiting your body. When you are able to feel present within the internal space of your body, you can proceed to the instructions for attuning to the pervasive space of fundamental consciousness inside and outside of your body at the same time.

Before you practice the Attunement to Fundamental Consciousness exercise below, it may be helpful to practice the following brief exercise for feeling the difference between being aware of your body and inhabiting your body.

It may also help you to do the practices in this book if you record yourself reading them so that you can follow the instructions in your own voice.

Being Aware of Your Body vs. Inhabiting Your Body

Sit with your back straight. Rest your hands in your lap. Take a few moments to become aware of your hands. As you do this, you may experience the temperature of your hands, how hot or cold they are. You may experience how relaxed or tense they are. You may also notice that you are experiencing your hands from outside of them. Now enter into your hands, inhabit them. Feel that you *are* the internal space of your hands. Feel that you are living and present within your hands.

Attunement to Fundamental Consciousness

Sit with your back straight. You can do this practice with your eyes open or closed, whichever is more comfortable for you.

Breathe evenly in and out through your nose. Let your breath be smooth and calm.

Bring your focus down to your feet. Feel that you are inside your feet, that you inhabit your feet. You are not just aware of your feet; feel that you *are* the internal space of your feet. Make sure that you can stay in your feet as you breathe, that your inhale does not lift you up away from your feet. Attune to the quality of self, a particular quality that feels like self, inside your feet. This is not an idea; it is a feeling.

Now feel that you are inside your ankles and your lower legs. Attune to the quality of self inside your ankles and lower legs.

Feel that you are inside your knees. Balance your awareness of the space inside your knees, finding both those internal areas at the same time. Experience the stillness of the balanced mind.

Feel that you are inside your thighs. Settle deeply within your thighs, from your knees to your hip sockets. Attune to the quality of self inside your thighs.

Feel that you are inside your hip sockets, with a very subtle mind, a "thin" mind. From the inside of your hip sockets, you may be able to feel the internal space of your upper thighs and the internal space of your lower torso at the same time. Balance your awareness of the space inside your hip sockets, finding the inside of both hip sockets at the same time. Experience the stillness of your balanced mind and the movement of your breath at the same time.

Feel that you are inside your pelvis. Let yourself settle into your pelvis so that you feel comfortable living in your pelvis. Attune to the quality of your gender inside your pelvis, however that feels to you. Again, this is not an idea but a feeling. It does not have to feel particularly male or female—let yourself experience however it feels to you. Bring your breath down into your pelvis and let it pass through the quality of gender inside your pelvis. (Please note: you can leave out this part of the exercise if inhabiting your pelvis and/or attuning to the quality of gender are not comfortable for you.)

Now inhabit your whole pelvic floor, including the sitz bones. Let your breath adjust to you being that far down in your body so that your inhale does not lift you up away from there.

Find a point in front of the base of your spine, on the bottom of your torso. Open this area and allow a current of energy to rise up from this point into your pelvis. Do not pull this energy up or visualize it; allow it to come up by itself. This is a very slender current—a thread of energy. Be patient with this. It may take some practice of inhabiting your body before you can feel this upward current.

Inhabit your midsection, between your ribs and your pelvis, including the solar plexus area under the ribs. Attune to the quality of your power, your personal strength, inside your midsection. Bring your breath down into your midsection and let it pass through the quality of power inside that area.

Find a point in the innermost core of your midsection, as deeply inward as you can focus without strain. Open this point and receive the upward-moving current of energy into your midsection. Let it come up by itself.

Inhabit your chest, all the way through to your back so that you are even inhabiting your upper back, and out to both sides of your chest. Attune to the quality of love inside your chest. This does not need to be a strong feeling; just a little of the tenderness that you may be able to feel within your chest. Bring your breath down into your chest and let it pass through the quality of love there. Let yourself settle in your chest so that you feel that you are sitting in your heart.

Find a point in the innermost core of your chest. Open this point and receive the upward-moving current of energy inside your chest. This upward current still comes from the bottom of your torso.

Inhabit your shoulders so that they feel soft at the edges. Attune to the quality of self inside your shoulders. Feel that you are inside your shoulder sockets with a very subtle, thin mind. From the inside of your shoulder sockets, you can feel the internal space of your upper arms and the internal space of your upper torso at the same time. Balance your awareness of the space inside your shoulder sockets, finding the inside of both shoulder sockets at the same time. Experience the stillness of the balanced mind and your breath moving through that stillness without disturbing it or changing it in any way.

Inhabit your arms, wrists, and hands all the way to your fingertips. Attune to the quality of self inside your arms, wrists, and hands.

Inhabit your neck. Let yourself settle within your neck. Experience yourself living within your whole neck, including your larynx. Attune to the quality of your voice, your potential to speak, inside your neck. Bring your breath down into your neck and let it pass through the quality of your voice inside your neck. Find a point in the innermost core of your neck. Open this point and receive the upward-moving current of energy into your neck.

Feel that you are inside your whole forehead, all the way around to the temples. Let your forehead soften and relax. Find a point in the center of your forehead (not between the brows but in the center of your forehead). Keep this point steady as you breathe. It may move around with your inhale and exhale; see what you need to let go of for the point to be steady as you breathe.

Now get back behind that point so that you are seeing it from behind, from deep inside your head. Let yourself see whatever is there. If it is a dark cave, let yourself see into the darkness without moving toward it. With practice, you may see a point, or a pearl, of light there. Focusing on the point within your forehead may help you open the subtle range of your vision.

Now inhabit your eyes. Let your eyes soften so that they feel continuous with the rest of your face. Feel that you are behind your cheekbones and inside your nose, all the way to its tip. Feel that you are inside your jaw, your mouth, your lips, and your chin. Feel that you are inside your ears, right through their centers (not too high up).

Inhabit your whole brain. Attune to the quality of your understanding, what that feels like, inside your whole brain. Bring your breath straight back through your head on your inhale and let it release on the exhale. Experience the breath moving through the quality of understanding inside your head.

Find your head center. This is in the innermost depth of the internal space of your head (not your forehead or the top of your head). Let this point settle and receive the upward-moving current of energy into your head. The energy still comes from the bottom of your torso. Now you can let the energy continue to pass upward and out through the top of your head. But do not go with the movement of energy. Just experience the energy moving through you. The top of your head needs to be gently settled for the energy to move up through it.

Feel that you are inside your whole body all at once. If we say that the body is the temple, you are sitting inside the temple, with nothing left out. To inhabit your body means to be in contact with yourself everywhere in your body at once.

Attune to the quality of self in your whole body. Feel that you are made of the quality of self.

Keeping your eyes closed (if they are closed), find the space outside of your body, the space in the room. Experience that the space inside your body and the space outside your body is the same continuous, undivided space. It pervades you.

You are still inside your body, but your body is permeable, pervaded by space. Let yourself experience that you *are* the space of fundamental consciousness. It is not something separate from you. It feels like who you are.

Slowly open your eyes (if they were closed). Feel that you are inside your whole body at once. Attune to the quality of self in your whole body. Even though the world appears, you still have the same internal depth, the same temple to sit inside.

Find the space outside your body and once again experience that the space inside and outside of your body is the same continuous expanse of space. It pervades you—not as movement but as an undivided stillness inside and out. Experience your breath passing easily through the space of your body.

Let yourself experience that you *are* the space of fundamental consciousness. Experience that the space pervading your body also pervades your whole environment. But you are still inside your whole body as you experience this. Do not project yourself out into your environment. Attune to the space that seems to already be there, pervading you and your environment. You do not have to move at all in order to do this.

Experience that the space pervading your body also pervades the walls of the room. Remain inside your whole body while you experience the space pervading you and the walls of the room. You are not finding the walls; you are finding the space that pervades you and the walls of the room.

Sit for a few moments, or as long as is comfortable, with your eyes open, attuned to the space of fundamental consciousness pervading you and your environment. As fundamental consciousness, you can let go of your grasp on yourself and your environment. Let everything be just as it is in the moment.

This practice is an attunement to fundamental consciousness. It is not yet the realization of fundamental consciousness. It cultivates the inward focus and the refinement of your consciousness that are necessary to facilitate the natural arising of fundamental consciousness. After each practice session, let go of the volitional attunement to fundamental consciousness and just sit for a few moments, or as long as is comfortable.

As you sit, you may be able to let go and relax into the pervasive consciousness that you have just attuned to. But rather than letting go from the surface of yourself, you can let go from within the whole internal depth of your body—not by leaving your body but by opening right there within your body.

People sometimes ask me what this letting go feels like. It feels just the same as if we were holding on to an object and we let go of it, we let it go from our grasp. In this way, we are gradually letting go of the protective grasp on ourselves that we have been holding since childhood. We are letting go of our constricting grip on our capacity for emotion, physical sensation, cognition, and perception. Some of these constrictions are so deeply ingrained, so tightly held, that they will not let go just by inhabiting the internal space of the body. They will need to be worked with directly, and their psychological purpose revealed and resolved. But to some extent, we can let go of our habitual hold on ourselves—our habitual diminishment of ourselves—and settle into the pervasive space of fundamental consciousness just by contacting and inhabiting the internal space of our body.

You may notice that in this practice, I use the terms *space* and *fundamental consciousness* interchangeably. This is because we experience fundamental consciousness as spaciousness, as an undivided expanse of space, pervading our body and environment. But this is not physical space. It is the spacious expanse of fundamental consciousness. I also use the term *ground* or *ground of being* to describe this same fundamental aspect of ourselves. This is because fundamental consciousness is experienced as the foundation, the essence of ourselves, that we uncover rather than create.

TO FACILITATE YOUR PRACTICE

When you practice the Attunement to Fundamental Consciousness, there are several things to notice. Be sure that you are actually present within your body rather than just aware of your body. As you inhabit your body, you may notice that some parts are easier for you to inhabit than other parts. Most people experience this. It just indicates your particular design of openness and constriction. If there are parts of your body that you cannot access at all, you can skip those parts and just continue with the rest of the instructions. If there are parts of your body that you can inhabit somewhat but are still challenging for you to access, then you can choose to dwell a little longer in those more challenging parts. As you continue to practice, you will gradually be able to increase your internal contact with yourself. The reason that these are called "practices" is that they are meant to bring you gradually into the experiences they aim for, with repeated practice, over time.

The pattern of openness and constriction in the body is often experienced as a difference between inhabiting the right and left sides of the body. Often that design is complex—we may live more in one part of the left side of our body and more in another part of the right side of our body. Balancing your awareness of the matching points in the body can begin to balance the way you inhabit it. But it is important not to try to hold on to that balance. Just attune to it and then let it go. Gradually that will help shift you toward inhabiting both sides of your body equally. If you find that you are shifting your focus back and forth between the matching areas, you need to make your mind more subtle, to "thin" it out, to find both at the same time. It can also help to find first one side, then the other, then both at once. For example: find your right shoulder socket, then find your left shoulder socket, then find both shoulder sockets at the same time.

As you inhabit each part of your body, let yourself settle within it. This is not a collapse, but an internal settling. The settling down in your body will help you experience your internal coherence—the undivided continuity within your body. Also, the more settled you are within your body, the more easily the upward current will rise through the core of your body.

Some people say that they experience the upward current as a big "whoosh" rather than a slender thread of energy. It is good to experience the upward current in any form, but the more slender it is, the more subtle it is. In this practice, we want the upward current to be as subtle as possible, to feel like a slender thread of energy. To experience this very subtle energy means that we have reached our deepest, most subtle inward attunement with the core of our being. So if you experience that upward whoosh of energy, try to refine your attunement to it so that you can experience the slender current.

Experiencing the upward current is the most challenging part of the practice for many people. When you find each point in the core of yourself, it can help to settle the point, to let the point rest within your body, to receive the upward current. You can also feel that you are making room for the upward current within the core of yourself.

Usually, experiencing the upward current just requires patience and continued practice. But it may also be that you are opening to it too far forward at the base of your torso. Try finding the bottom of your torso a little farther back, right in front of the base of your spine, and opening to it there. You may feel that the upward current is fragmented, that you can feel it move in parts of your core but not through the whole core. Again, it is just a matter of patience and continued methodical practice for you to experience the upward current as a continuous flow.

People also sometimes report an experience of trembling or quaking as they inhabit their body. This generally happens spontaneously when a part of your body that has been very tense suddenly opens. It is not something to be concerned about, but it is also not something to try to induce. Some contemporary Hindu teachers encouraged this quaking, or kriyas, as a sign of progress toward spiritual realization. Also, some body-oriented psychotherapy modalities, such as bioenergetic therapy, specifically teach people to hold their bodies in extreme positions so that their muscles tremble and release. But in the Realization Process, we are working on a level of stillness that is more subtle than energetic trembling or quaking. If you just allow the trembling to occur without either suppressing or exaggerating it, you will gradually settle into that stillness and the trembling, quaking movements will cease to occur.

At the end of the practice, when you attune to the space pervading your body and environment, take care that you are not leaving your body to do this. To experience the oneness of fundamental consciousness, you need to attune to it pervading your own body and your environment at the same time. This is not an energetic expansion outward but a settling inward that allows for the attunement to pervasive space.

THE QUALITIES WITHIN THE BODY

The innate—unconstructed—nature of the qualities that we can discover within our body is, for me, one of the great mysteries of our existence. These qualities, such as the actual feel of power in our belly and the feel of love in our chest, are naturally uncovered as we inhabit the internal space of our body. They may be challenging to experience at first, but they will eventually emerge as you continue to deepen your contact with the internal space of your body.

Attuning to the qualities within the body helps us experience that fundamental consciousness is the ground of our own being, the foundation of our human nature. It is also these qualities that we have shut down in response to painful events in our childhood. For example, when we feel overpowered by an abusive adult or a bullying peer, we may diminish our own power in response and lose the ability to experience the feeling of power in our belly. As we open to these innate qualities of our being, we feel that we are actually made of love, that we are made of power, of voice, of understanding, and for some of us, of sexuality and gender (however that feels to each of us). These are the characteristics of our experience of authentic, unfragmented, unobstructed being. Even though each quality can be opened to most easily in specific parts of the body, as instructed in the above practice, they can all be experienced pervading our whole body and being. This is much easier to experience than to grasp intellectually. As fundamental consciousness, we can experience ourselves as a blend of these innate qualities of our being, everywhere in our body.

The easiest quality for most people to experience is the quality of love. The love that emerges as you live within the space of your chest does not require an object. It is always there within your body, and you can access it at any time. Experiencing the quality of love within our body even when we are alone can help us overcome feelings of loneliness and abandonment.

Many people feel an aversion to the quality of power. Traditionally, women have been taught that it is not feminine, and therefore not attractive, for a woman to embody power. Even if we have not been taught that limitation directly, it may be passed down from one generation to the next, as girls mirror the constriction of power in their mothers. Men also sometimes constrict their quality of power because of gender stereotypes—not wanting to be the negative stereotype of a man who uses his power to dominate, abuse, or intimidate. But the power that resides naturally in your midsection is not the power over someone. It is "good" power, like the power of a waterfall. It is good power because it is your power, and you can choose how to use it. And it is also good because it is balanced by your love and your understanding that also reside in your body.

The quality of gender is also problematic for many people and often the most difficult for people to attune to. The instruction is to attune to the quality of gender "however that feels to you" because the practice does not suggest that your experience be specifically male or female or that it match your biological gender. It is whatever you experience as the quality within your own pelvis. And as mentioned in the exercise, you can also leave out inhabiting your pelvis and/or attuning to the quality of gender, if that part of the exercise is not comfortable for you.

The quality of gender has nothing to do with the stereotypical limitations that culture has assigned to men and women. It is a quality, a feeling, not an idea. As a quality of the ground of our being, it is completely without content.

It has become popular to deny that there is any such thing as gender, that gender is only a social construct. People sometimes react to the word *gender* as they react to the word *self*—as if it is a bad word. My sense is that this reaction is part of our culture's gender wound. It is part of our healthy rebellion against those social conventions that have kept people from being whole human beings, but it can also limit us from experiencing all of the qualities of our being.

I know that this is a sensitive topic, and the controversy surrounding it is an important issue for our culture, for our recognition and encouragement of personal freedom, and our battle against bigotry. However, I have kept this instruction in the Realization Process because I have found that for some people, to actually experience the feel of gender within their body can be a remedy for the limitations and distortions of socially constructed gender. For some of us, it can help us heal our fragmentations, even our own self-loathing, based on our dislike for our own gender.

We may suppress the feel of our gender within our body either because we have accepted as truth the limiting social construction of gender or because we fear becoming the negative images of male and female that we see around us, in our lives and in the media. We may also have shut down the feel of gender because of trauma, even abuse, that we have suffered based on our gender.

If we have created constrictions in our pelvis to suppress the feel of gender, those constrictions can limit our capacity for sexual arousal and pleasure. I have also found that some people are unable to experience the quality of gender because of constrictions that they created in reaction to sexual trauma. This means that for some of us, to regain that part of ourselves, to be able to comfortably live within our pelvis and experience the quality of our being within our pelvis, can help us recover from both our social and trauma-based personal wounds. But in including this part of the Realization Process in this book, I am trusting the reader, as I trust my students, to use only those practices that feel helpful and healing for you and to skip those that do not.

7

Steadiness

This vast expanse, unwavering, indescribable, and equal to
space, is timelessly and innately present in all beings.

—Longchen Rabjam

Fundamental consciousness is experienced as stillness. When we
realize it, we uncover an unwavering, unchanging expanse of
space within all of the movement of life. There is a gentleness
in this stillness, a calm, an inner peace that we can each experience
within our own being and within everything around us.

As fundamental consciousness, our body is suffused with this
gentle stillness. We feel that we are made of stillness that is always
there within all of the changing thoughts, feelings, and sensations
within our body. And that stillness within our body is continuous
with the stillness that pervades everywhere in our experience of
our environment. When we move through space, stillness moves
through stillness.

As I attempt to describe this, I am reminded of a poem by Rainer
Maria Rilke that ends with the words, "We are all falling. This hand
falls. / And look at others: it is in them all. / And yet there is one who
holds this falling / endlessly gently in his hands."[1] When we realize
the undivided ground of our being, we can experience that all of the
commotion of life, all of our striving and surging, reaching and falling
are held within one single, steady, and somehow gentle expanse.

Fundamental consciousness does not change. It cannot be fragmented or altered in any way, no matter how intense our circumstances. Therefore, it is unbreakable. It is the stable, unbreakable ground of our being, beyond injury, beyond psychological trauma. When we realize it, we know that no matter what we have suffered in our lives, no matter what we have lost or how much pain we have endured, this primary aspect of ourselves has survived intact. One of the great rewards of nondual realization is that we finally recognize that we have not been irreparably damaged by our life circumstances. We are still there; we can still find ourselves, whole and capable.

Fundamental consciousness is naturally still, without any effort on our part to create stillness. When we uncover it, we find a stillness that seems to have always been there.

Here is how Zen master Seung Sahn described it: "Everything in this world—the sun, the moon, the stars, mountains, rivers and trees—everything is constantly moving. But there is one thing that never moves. It never comes or goes. It is never born and never dies. What is this non-moving thing? Can you tell me? If you find that, you will find your true self and attain universal substance."[2]

As this undivided stillness, we are disentangled from the movement of life. Disentanglement is not detachment in the sense of disconnection or disassociation. It is nongrasping, nonobstruction. Our thoughts, emotions, physical sensations, and perceptions move freely through the disentangled stillness.

Knowing ourselves as fundamental consciousness provides a deepened perspective on the changing content of our experience, but at the same time it also brings us closer to our experience. It dissolves our habitual filters. We feel more deeply as fundamental consciousness. We know and perceive more clearly. It is as if for the first time we are truly seeing, truly touching. However, we also recognize that we are not this content, that our true identity is beyond these passing impressions. We can allow our perceptions and responses to flow and to change, to begin and end, as they move through the unchanging ground of our being.

This brings an underlying steadiness to our ongoing experience of life. We know ourselves as this same unwavering ground within the movement of any situation. This means that we can remain open and receptive in any situation. The unbreakable, disentangled nature of fundamental consciousness allows us to receive each moment of life in its full impact, without fear of overwhelm or annihilation.

NONDUAL PERCEPTION

This open receptivity is responsible for the enhanced vividness of perception that we experience as fundamental consciousness. Although there may still be some chronic protective patterns of constriction in our senses even after we have realized fundamental consciousness, we experience all of our sensory stimuli—everything seen, heard, smelled, tasted, and touched—as occurring in the pervasive space with greater clarity. This brightening and refining of the sensory world contributes to the sense of awakening that we experience with nondual realization. We awaken to the unobstructed vividness of the world around us.

The sensory stimuli in our environment are changing vibratory patterns that occur in the space, while our attunement to fundamental consciousness is unchanged and ongoing. In Zen Buddhism, they say, "The person sees the mountain, the mountain sees the person." Subject and object are completely integrated. The seer, the seeing, and the seen have become a single, simultaneous event.

BALANCE

Since fundamental consciousness is experienced as unwavering stillness, it can be described as the dimension of perfect balance or symmetry. Human beings have an innate sense of symmetry and balance. We can discern it visually and audibly, as harmony, and we can feel it in our body. Balance is the basis of ease and comfort; imbalance is the basis of discomfort, confusion, and pain.

Artists make use of this sense of balance to convey beauty or, in some more contemporary art, to express disharmony, to create in the audience a sense of disorientation. When we see or hear a portrayal of balance, we feel a kind of satisfaction. It may be because we all have within us this underlying ground of stillness and perfect balance, that art can, to some extent, fulfill the common human yearning to transcend the disharmony of ordinary life.

THE RED BALL

I sometimes play a game with my students to help them experience the unbreakable steadiness of fundamental consciousness. I sit facing the student, close up, our knees almost touching. I ask them to inhabit their body and to attune to fundamental consciousness pervading us both.

Then I hold out my empty palm and I say, "I have an imaginary red ball around the size of a pea, and I am going to toss it over each of your shoulders. Just let it pass through." They often respond to this with an indulgent smile. After all, there is nothing but empty space above their shoulders, and the ball is imaginary. What could go wrong?

Then I gently toss it over each of their shoulders, and usually, at first, it does not pass through. For the movement of the ball is not entirely imaginary. My action of tossing it creates a slight vibration. And either the space around them is too dense, too thick, for the passage of that vibration, or they quickly produce a density to stop its movement. They do this by tightening within their body, which creates a density, not just within their body but also in the space around them.

To understand this better, take a moment to try to block your hearing of the sounds in your environment. You may not be able to actually block the sounds, but you may be able to feel what you do within your body, and even in the space around your body, in order to attempt to block the sounds. This is a natural protective mechanism that we all possess. Just as we can constrict our hearing against the sound of angry voices or tighten our solar plexus area against the feeling of anxiety, we can block the space around us against the vibration of the ball's trajectory. These protective movements, when repeated over time, become the chronic rigidities in our body that obstruct our ability to inhabit our body and realize fundamental consciousness.

And that chronic or sudden density in the space around my student, when I toss the ball over their shoulder, is visible. When we realize ourselves as fundamental consciousness, our perception, as I have said, becomes more subtle. This allows us to be able to see when a person's body, and the space around them, is open and when it is blocked, and even to perceive a person's particular pattern of chronic constriction that they have held, usually since childhood.

Often the student will stop and hold the imaginary ball (the vibration of its movement) midway in its passage as if to analyze its nature—is it friend or foe?—before allowing it to continue in its movement. They do this automatically and unconsciously. It can take several tosses of the red ball before they are able to recognize and let go of these protective tactics and reach a more subtle attunement to themselves—to the disentangled stillness of fundamental consciousness that allows for clear passage of the ball. As fundamental consciousness, we do not need protective tactics because no stimuli, no matter how abrasive it is, can injure or shatter the ground of our being.

When they can allow the red ball to pass over their shoulders without obstructing it, I then toss the ball not above but through each of their shoulders. They are often surprised that even within the substance of their body they can find the empty unbreakable stillness that allows the ball to pass through them.

Once they can open to the free flow of the imaginary ball, they are ready for the "supermarket challenge," or any place or situation in which they can practice allowing the vibrations, the movement of life, to pass through the disentangled stillness of their attunement to fundamental consciousness. Again, this is not detachment. We may respond deeply to whatever stimuli pass through us. We may allow stimuli to pass through without responding to them, or we may take in and savor something that nourishes us, such as the touch or gaze of someone we love. We can surrender to the influence of pleasurable stimuli, and we can choose to focus our attention on some stimuli and ignore others. We can even still block stimuli, consciously, without losing our realization of fundamental consciousness. No matter what our response to it is, no event can disturb our contact with the undivided ground of our being when we know ourselves as that ground.

If you would like to try this out: Inhabit your body. Find the space outside of your body, the space in your environment. Attune to the space pervading you and your whole environment. Everything that you experience, both within and outside of your body, is pervaded by fundamental consciousness. If there are sounds, let them move through the space without changing the stillness of the space. If there is movement, such as tree branches moving in the wind outside your window, or an animal or a person moving through your room, let the movement occur in the space without disrupting your attunement to the pervasive stillness. If you feel pleasure, or some other emotion, let it move freely through the unchanging ground of your being. Let yourself experience that this whole unfolding moment is held, effortlessly, in the steady, undivided stillness of fundamental consciousness.

8

Cultivating Steadiness

The following meditation is the main Realization Process practice for opening to the unwavering stillness of fundamental consciousness. Fundamental consciousness is always still, but your attunement to it can waver. Usually, when you find your attunement to fundamental consciousness wavering, it is because either your perceptual field or your breath is not disentangled sufficiently from the pervasive expanse of fundamental consciousness. The stillness of fundamental consciousness pervades your breath and all of your internal experience, and it pervades your sensory experience of your surroundings.

Steadiness Meditation

Sit upright with your eyes open. Rest your gaze on the floor in front of you (without bending your head forward) or focus straight ahead.

Inhabit your whole body. Find the space outside of your body. Experience that the space inside and outside of your body is the same continuous expanse of space. Experience that the space that pervades your body pervades your whole environment. Remain within your body as you attune to this.

Breathe calmly and gently through your nose. Your breath moves through the stillness of fundamental consciousness without disturbing or altering the stillness. The stillness of fundamental consciousness pervades the movement of your breath.

Sit for five minutes, or as long as you are comfortable, opening to the unwavering nature of the pervasive space of fundamental consciousness. Do not hold the space still but open into the stillness that is already there, pervading your body and environment.

The next practices can be done in any order. They can help you open to and stabilize in the stillness of fundamental consciousness. It can be helpful, after each of the following practices, to sit for a few minutes in the Steadiness Meditation.

ABOUT NONDUAL PERCEPTION

When we know ourselves as fundamental consciousness, our senses become more unified and more subtle. It feels as if fundamental consciousness is doing the perceiving. This is a nongrasping, an unguarded reception of our sensory experience. In the Realization Process, we practice experiencing the change that occurs in our senses with nondual realization so that our old organization of subject-object fragmentation does not reassert itself as soon as we interact with our environment.

The following practice guides you to see and hear "as the space" of fundamental consciousness. This does not mean that there are "sounds without a hearer" or "sights without a seer." It is still we ourselves who are seeing and hearing. But we are perceiving as the space of fundamental consciousness, disentangled from the perceptual stimuli. If we try to separate the perceiver from the perceived, we create a fragmentation in ourselves that is the opposite of the self-other unity of nondual realization.

Nondual perception is not a fixated external focus on the world around us with a collapse of our internal experience. It arises out of the consciousness that is the ground of our internal and external experience, as a unity. For that reason, we can have a clear perception of the world around us and an internal response to that perception at the same time. Even if we dislike an object, or if the object evokes a profuse internal monologue, we can still perceive the object as fundamental consciousness.

As you practice nondual perception, be careful not to project yourself into the objects of your perception. Remain in your body, attuned to the space that pervades you and the objects of your perception at the same time.

As mentioned earlier, most people have chronic constriction in their bodies—constriction that once served a protective purpose. Most people have constriction in their senses, usually created in childhood, to protect against overwhelming stimuli or to concentrate or as a result of straining to be more alert to their environment. As you practice seeing as fundamental consciousness, you may find that some of the chronic constrictions in your eyes release. You may find that your eyes feel unfocused as they let go of these tensions. With continued practice, your eyes will refocus in a more relaxed way. But do not volitionally blur your perception as you do this practice. This is not meant to be a soft focus, although it may feel soft compared to the effort that many of us make to see.

There are four parts to the practice of nondual perception. They are not meant to be done at the same time. But you should do the first part of the practice (A) before going on to the others. Then the next three can be done at different times, in any order. They will each contribute to your ability to remain attuned to fundamental consciousness as you perceive your environment.

Practicing Nondual Perception

A. Sit with your eyes open. Breathe smoothly and evenly through your nose. Inhabit your feet. Let your breath adjust to you being in your feet so that your inhale does not lift you up away from your feet. Inhabit your whole body, including your feet. Find the space outside of your body, the space in the room. Experience that the space inside and outside your body is the same continuous expanse of space. It pervades you. Experience that the space that pervades your body also pervades your whole environment. Remain in your whole body as you experience this.

Experience that all of the sounds you hear are occurring in the space of fundamental consciousness without changing the space.

Experience that the space itself is hearing the sounds. The space pervades the sounds. You do not have to listen in order to hear. Receive the sounds without any effort.

Now allow everything that you see to be in the space of fundamental consciousness without changing or altering the space. The visuals arise directly out of the space.

Experience that the space itself is doing the seeing. The space pervades the objects. You do not have to look in order to see. Receive the visuals without any effort.

Experience that the sounds and the visuals both occur in the space of fundamental consciousness without changing the stillness of the space. The space is hearing and seeing without any effort to listen or look. Receive the sounds and visuals at the same time.

B. Choose an object in your environment and sit in front of it. Inhabit your whole body. Attune to the space pervading you and the object. Note that this is not the space between you and the object—the space pervades both you and the object. With practice, you will be able to experience the mutual "transparency" of yourself and the object. It is not that you can actually see through the object to what is behind it. It is an experience that both you and the object are pervaded by and made of the same continuous expanse of pervasive fundamental consciousness. Experience that the space of fundamental consciousness is seeing the object. The space pervades and reveals the object without any effort on your part. This is a nongrasping, a reception of the visual experience.

C. Listen to a piece of music that you enjoy. Inhabit your whole body. Attune to the space pervading you and your whole environment. Let the space do the hearing. The sounds will move through the space, even through the space of your body. Stay attuned to the pervasive stillness of fundamental consciousness as the music moves through it.

D. Sit in front of a moving object, such as trees moved by the wind or steam rising off a pot of boiling water. Inhabit your whole body. Attune to the space pervading you and the moving object. Stay attuned to the unwavering stillness of fundamental consciousness and allow the movement to pass through the stillness without disturbing or altering the stillness in any way.

BALANCE AND STILLNESS

Fundamental consciousness is experienced as stillness because it is the dimension of perfect balance. One of the ways that we enter into this stillness is by meditating on the balance of points within our body. If it is difficult for you to find both matching points at the same time— if you are going back and forth between the points—it means that you need to refine or "thin out" your mind. As previously mentioned, it can help to find the left one, then the right one, then both at the same time. There is a subtle vibration, a kind of "spark" or "ring" when you find both points simultaneously.

Attuning to Balance

Sit or stand with your eyes closed. If you feel uncomfortable standing with your eyes closed, you can support yourself by resting your hands gently on the back of a chair.

Inhabit your feet. Let your breath adjust to you being that far down in your body so that your inhale does not lift you up away from your feet. Inhabit your whole body, including your feet. Breathe smoothly and calmly through your nose.

Find the centers of the soles of your heels. Balance your awareness of these two points. Find them both at the same time. Dwell for a few moments in the balanced awareness of the centers of the soles of your heels.

Find the inside of your hip sockets. Balance your awareness of the space inside both hip sockets. Find them both at the same time. Dwell for a few moments in the balanced awareness of the space inside your hip sockets.

Find the inside of your shoulder sockets. Balance your awareness of these two points. Find them both at the same time. Dwell for a few moments in the balanced awareness of the space inside your shoulder sockets.

Find the space outside of each of your ears. Balance your awareness of the space outside of your ears. Find both those places at the same time. Dwell for a few moments in the balanced awareness of the space outside of both of your ears.

Find the centers of the palms of your hands. Balance your awareness of the centers of your palms. Find both those points at the same time. Dwell for a few moments in the balanced awareness of the centers of your palms.

Inhabit your whole body. Feel that you are completely one with the internal space of your body.

Open your eyes. Continue to feel completely one with the internal space of your body. Breathe smoothly and calmly through your nose.

9

Depth

The "mind" here is not the surface consciousness, but the "mind"
that penetrates into the body and deeply subjectivizes it.

—Yasuo Yuasa

One of the most valuable gifts of nondual realization is the
experience of depth. Inhabiting our whole body as fundamental consciousness, we can feel our aliveness all the way
through the internal volume of our body.

This inward contact is the basis of our ability to be alone with ourselves in the innermost depth of our mind and heart, to feel private
and removed from the influence of our surroundings. It is also the
basis of our ability to be engaged and responsive, to be moved and
excited from this same depth by people and events in our environment.

To the extent that we can experience inward contact with ourselves, we can also feel depth of contact with the life around us. We
can see, feel, and touch beyond the surface of plant, animal, and
human forms to the life within them. In chapter 15, I will describe
the mutual contact that we can experience with other people who
have also realized fundamental consciousness.

However, fundamental consciousness is not just the basis of our
contact with living forms but with all forms in our environment, even
inanimate objects. Fundamental consciousness pervades everywhere, to
the edges of our perception, and we experience contact throughout the

whole undivided expanse of our perception. This is because fundamental consciousness, pervading our whole body as well as our environment, is not just a perceptual experience. As the ground of our whole being, there is a subtle emotional and tactile component to the realization of fundamental consciousness. Without moving from within our own body, we can know, see, feel, and touch the internal depth of everything within the reach of our perception. In the Realization Process, we call this blend of perception and contact a "see-feel."

This inward contact with our body and outward contact with our environment is not a movement inward or outward. It is the stable expanse of our contact with ourselves and our world as fundamental consciousness. Far from being the detached, zombie-like state that some nondual teachings describe, nondual realization increases our intimacy with our own being and with everything and everyone that we encounter. Nondual realization is therefore not a state without pain. If our experience at times is not so lovely, if there are abrasive sounds, smells, and sights, or if there is suffering within our view, and if we are very sensitive, even beyond the scope of our ordinary sensory perception or within our own being, we will know them as well with the same blend of perception and contact. Although our realization of fundamental consciousness can prevent us from being shattered by painful events in our lives, it in no way limits our ability to feel and respond to those events.

SPATIAL DEPTH

The depth of experience that occurs as we realize fundamental consciousness can be understood in two ways. One is as spatial depth— the ability to know, sense, and connect inwardly to the core of ourselves and outwardly to the periphery of our experience of our environment. The second way to understand depth is as the fullness, or breadth, of experience.

Nonduality naturally provides spatial depth to our experience because it requires that we access and live within the internal space of our body, including the subtle channel that runs through the innermost vertical core of our body. As I mentioned in chapter 4, this subtle channel is situated from the bottom of our torso, right in front of the base of our spine, and runs to the top of our head. We experience it even more deeply within ourselves than the midline of our body. It is behind the midline. It is one of our main entranceways into the pervasive, unified space of fundamental consciousness. The more contact we have with this channel, the more complete is our realization.

The subtle core of the body is also important for our personal maturity. When we live within this core, we feel our deepest connection with our individual being. Although this core is our entranceway into self-other oneness, to live within it feels like our greatest distance from our environment, and our deepest perspective on both our internal and external experience. Even our visual perspective is deepened as we reach this core of ourselves.

From within this core, we can most easily let go of our habitual, controlling grip on our understanding, emotions, sensations, and perceptions. We can allow life to be as it is in each moment, and we can allow life to flow and to change. We feel that we are living in the center of all our experience, responsive and yet disentangled from the changing content and movement of the world around us. We can respond to that world, but we are not caught up in our habitual reactive patterns of response to other people and events.

We also become more evenly aligned within our body. To a sensitive observer, someone who is just beginning to do inward practices looks a little like a cubist painting, with parts of themselves jutting out in different directions, out of alignment with other parts of themselves. As we are able to access more of our core, we look smoother and more coherent, like a stone that has been worn smooth by the sea.

At this core of ourselves, we have access to all of our internal resources for responding to our surroundings. We can relate from what feels like the source of our love, the source of our insight, and the source of our personal strength and will. In the core of our being, we can even access an innate wellspring of happiness that is not dependent on our circumstances.

BREADTH

The second way that nondual realization deepens our experience of ourselves and our world is that it engages and integrates the full breadth of our human capacities. The pervasive expanse of fundamental consciousness can be experienced as emptiness, as the clear-through permeability of our body and environment. But this same pervasive transparency can also be experienced as containing the full range of the subtle qualities of our humanness. In the Realization Process we attune directly to the qualities of awareness, emotion, and physical sensation as the primary, unchanging qualities of fundamental consciousness. These are not specific awarenesses, emotions, or sensations that are always changing. They are the qualities that constitute the rich stillness of fundamental consciousness.

Just as there is a long-standing debate among nondual spiritual traditions regarding the existence of a ground of being, there is also an ongoing debate concerning whether or not this ground has qualities. Some spiritual teachings describe ultimate consciousness as being completely without qualities, and some claim that it does have inherent qualities that can be experienced. Yogic and Vedantic philosophies call these qualities sat, chit, ananda, which are typically translated as truth (or existence), intelligence, bliss.[1]

Shankara wrote, "Realize that to be Brahman which is Existence, Knowledge-Bliss Absolute, which is non-dual and infinite eternal and One, and which fills all that exists between."[2] Tibetan Buddhism describes nondual realization as the uncompounded union of emptiness, luminosity, and bliss.[3]

In the Realization Process, we are not making claims about the ultimate nature of reality. We attune to these primary qualities of fundamental consciousness experientially in order to open to it with our whole being. The reason that I use the term *consciousness* to denote the primary ground of being rather than *awareness,* as many nondual teachers do, is because I have found that the teaching of nondual awareness often causes people to only open to nonduality from above their neck. But if we do not open to fundamental consciousness with our whole being, we do not reach the experience of a subtle ground pervading everywhere.

In presenting awareness, emotion, and physical sensation as qualities of fundamental consciousness, I am not pointing to an awareness of our emotions and physical sensations. I am saying that when we open to fundamental consciousness with our whole body, we can experience awareness, emotion, and physical sensation as qualities inherent in the space itself.

When people meditate without attuning to the aspects of fundamental consciousness that I call awareness, emotion, and physical sensation, they tend to dwell in the part of themselves that is already most open, where they habitually live. This means that their meditation continues to cultivate the aspect of themselves that is already most developed. As time goes by, this exacerbates the fragmentation and imbalance that they began with and can become uncomfortable or overwhelming. For example, someone who is very open emotionally will generally dwell in their chest as they meditate. Over time, they may begin to feel overwhelmed by their emotional responses to life. They need to balance this emotional openness with awareness and physical sensation. Someone who lives more abstractly, approaching life primarily as something to analyze and understand, will usually dwell in their head, or more likely, in their forehead, as they meditate. After years of meditation practice, they may have an increased sense of mental clarity, but they will also feel increasingly cut off from their emotions and sensations.

In the Realization Process, we open to fundamental consciousness as the blend of awareness, emotion, and physical sensation. Although each of these qualities is entered into through specific parts of the body, as you will see in the next chapter, they all pervade our whole body and environment as an uncompounded integration. As fundamental consciousness, we perceive, feel, know, and move as that blend of qualities.

10

Cultivating Depth

The following practice can help you access and live within the subtle channel that runs through the innermost vertical core of your torso, neck, and head. This channel is referred to in the Realization Process as the "subtle core" of your body. In this practice, you will find three points within the subtle core of your body by focusing inwardly as deeply as you can, without strain.

The Core Breath

Sit upright, with your eyes closed.

Inhabit your feet. Make sure that you can continue to breathe while being in your feet—that your inhale does not lift you up away from your feet. Inhabit your whole body, including your feet.

Find your head center. This point is in the innermost core of the internal space of your head. (It is not the center of your forehead or the center of the top of your head.)

Just by being in your head center, you enter into your internal wholeness. You have access to everywhere in your body and being at once, without moving from your head center.

Inhale through your nose, bringing the breath into your head center. Exhale through your nose. The breath needs to be subtle or "thin" to move through your head.

Now, initiate the breath from within your head center so that your head center draws in the breath. It feels as if you have air in your head center that you can breathe. The exhale is a release from within your head center.

To initiate the breath within the point doesn't mean that you are bringing the breath to the core point or breathing into the point but rather that the breath starts within the point. The first place you feel the breath move, on both your inhale and your exhale, is within the core point. Although the breath will still come in through your nose, and it will still utilize your lungs, let yourself experience the movement of your breath within the point before you feel it move in your nose or your lungs.

By breathing within your head center, you can feel a resonance, a gentle vibration, throughout the whole subtle core of your body.

Find your heart center in the center of your chest but deep in the subtle core of the body. You can leave your head center now, and you are just in your heart center.

By being in your heart center, you enter into your wholeness. You have access to your whole internal body and being without moving from within your heart center.

Now initiate—draw in—the breath within your heart center. The exhale is a release from within your heart center. By breathing within your heart center, you can feel a resonance throughout the whole subtle core of your body.

Find your pelvic center in the center of your pelvis, deep in the subtle core of the body. (You can skip this part of the practice if it is uncomfortable for you to be in your pelvis. Just work with your head and heart centers.) Just by being in your pelvic center, you enter into your wholeness. You have access to your whole internal body and being without moving from within your pelvic center.

Initiate—draw in—the breath within your pelvic center. The exhale is a release from within the pelvic center. By breathing within your pelvic center, you can feel a resonance throughout the whole subtle core of your body.

Find your head center again. Find your head center and your heart center at the same time. Find all three centers at the same time.

Just by being in your head center, heart center, and pelvic center, you enter into your wholeness. You have access to your whole internal body and being.

Initiate the breath from within all three centers at the same time. The exhale is a release from within all three centers. By breathing within these three points, you can feel a gentle vibration throughout the whole internal space of your body.

Open your eyes and again find your head center, your heart center, and your pelvic center at the same time. By being in these three centers, you enter into your wholeness.

With your eyes open, initiate the breath from within all three centers at the same time. The exhale is a release from within all three centers. By breathing from within all three centers, you can feel a gentle vibration throughout the whole internal space of your body.

Experience your environment from this subtle core of your body. Usually we experience our environment from the surface of ourselves. When you shift to experiencing your surroundings from this core of yourself, it may deepen your visual perspective. Objects may seem farther away than usual. That is their true distance.

Find the space of fundamental consciousness pervading your body and environment. Sit for a moment, letting go from within each of the three core points into the space. Do not leave the core points to do this, but let go within the points, into the space.

HELP FOR BEGINNERS

If you are not able to find all three points at the same time, just find two. If you cannot initiate the breath within all three points at the same time, you can initiate your breath from two points. With practice, you will be able to add in the third point.

To help you experience initiating the breath within the core points, you can imagine someone placing a fingertip on your back, behind your heart center. Imagine the gentle touch of their fingertip and initiate your breath right where you feel that touch.

Most people start out by making the breath too big. The breath that is initiated within the points is a very fine (thin), subtle breath, like a thread of breath. Sometimes people feel that they cannot get enough air in the core breath. Even though the breath is very subtle and begins within the tiny core points, it can still be a long breath. This subtle core breath can fill your whole body.

You may also find that you are exerting too much or too little effort. This breath needs to be practiced gently and calmly. It requires very little effort, but it does require some. It is a gentle but volitional practice.

ADVANCED INSTRUCTIONS: THE MIND BREATHING

The mind breathing within the core points is an advanced instruction. In each point, as you initiate the breath, let yourself experience that the mind is breathing or that you are breathing a mixture of breath and mind.

You should not practice this until you are adept at initiating the breath within the points. The mind breathing has nothing to do with the thinking mind. It is just a textural change to the breath. It feels as if there is a very subtle, mental quality to the breath. You do not have to bring your mind or your awareness to the points to do this. Rather, it feels like the mind is already there within the points, breathing. This will refine your core breath and also refine the resonance, the gentle vibration that you can experience in your whole core and then everywhere in your body at once.

You can breathe within the subtle core of the body anywhere along it. For example, you can initiate the core breath within the point in front of the base of your spine or at the base of your neck or at the top of your head or even above your head. If you work with the upper points, always end your practice by inhabiting the whole core of your body down to the point in front of the base of your spine so that you do not become ungrounded. Then find the pervasive space of fundamental consciousness and let go from within the whole core into the space.

The next practice can help you cultivate the breadth aspect of fundamental consciousness.

The Qualities of Fundamental Consciousness

Sit upright with your eyes open.

Inhabit your feet. Let your breath adjust to you being in your feet so that your inhale does not lift you up away from your feet.

Inhabit your whole body, including your feet. Find the space outside your body, the space in the room. Experience that the space inside and outside your body is the same, continuous space. It pervades you. Experience that the space pervading your own body also pervades your whole environment. Do not move from within your body to do this; attune to the space that seems to already be there pervading you and your environment.

Attune to the quality of awareness within, around, and way above your head. Experience the quality of awareness pervading your whole body so that it feels like you are made of the quality of awareness. Experience the quality of awareness pervading your whole body and environment at the same time.

Attune to the quality of emotion in the middle of your body—your chest and gut. Experience the quality of emotion pervading your whole body so that it feels like you are made of the quality of emotion. This is not a specific emotion. It is the ground of emotion, like an emotional tone or color. As an aspect of the stillness of fundamental consciousness, it is unchanging and more subtle than any specific emotion. Experience the quality of emotion pervading your whole body and environment at the same time.

Come down into the bottom of your torso, legs, and feet and attune to the quality of physical sensation. Experience the quality of physical sensation pervading your whole body so that it feels like you are made of the quality of physical sensation. This is not a specific physical sensation. It is the subtle, unchanging ground of physical sensation. Experience the quality of physical sensation pervading your whole body and environment at the same time. This is the tactile quality of nondual realization. It feels as if you can touch the objects across the room from yourself, without moving from within your body. You may even feel as if you can touch within the objects because fundamental consciousness pervades the objects.

Now experience the quality of physical sensation pervading your whole body and environment and the quality of awareness pervading your whole body and environment at the same time.

Add the quality of emotion pervading your whole body and environment. At this point, the qualities blend together; you do not need to keep them distinct from each other.

Sit for a moment, or as long as is comfortable, in this rich field of awareness, emotion, and physical sensation pervading your body and environment.

———————————————

You may find at first that one or two of these qualities are easier for you to access than the others. This is a reflection of your particular design of openness and constriction and your habitual way of inhabiting your body. With practice, as you are able to more fully inhabit your body, you will be able to experience all three qualities of fundamental consciousness.

When you touch (or use any of your senses) as the blend of awareness, emotion, and physical sensation, your contact will contain both spatial depth and the fullness or breadth of experience.

Depth of Contact—Tactile

Place the palm of your hand on an object, such as a lamp. Attune to the quality of awareness in, around, and above your head. Feel that your whole body is made of awareness. Attune to the quality of awareness pervading you and the object. Touch the object as awareness.

Attune to the quality of emotion in your chest and gut. Feel that your whole body is made of emotion. Attune to the quality of emotion pervading you and the object. Touch the object as emotion.

Attune to the quality of physical sensation, low in your torso and legs. Feel that your whole body is made of physical sensation. Attune to the quality of physical sensation pervading you and the object. Touch the object as physical sensation.

Attune to awareness and physical sensation at the same time, pervading your whole body. Add the emotional quality pervading your whole body. The three qualities blend together. Feel that you are made of this blend of qualities. Attune to the rich space of awareness, emotion, and physical sensation pervading you and the object. Touch the object as the blend of awareness, emotion, and physical sensation.

You can do this same practice with a living being, such as a tree, or an animal or a person. Let yourself experience how touching as the blend of the three qualities deepens and enriches your contact with both physical objects and living beings. You may experience that you can touch all the way through the depth of an object. Especially with living beings, to touch or to be touched in this way is a true intimacy, a deepened, nonverbal knowing.

In this next practice, you may notice how seeing an object from the vantage point of each of these qualities changes what you perceive about the object. In chapter 5, I pointed out that the way we look out of our eyes corresponds to where we mainly inhabit our body. This placement of how we look out through our eyes means that we will see our environment mainly with, or as, the corresponding quality.

If we live more within the top of our body, we look out through the top third of our eyes, and we see our environment mostly from the vantage of awareness. This perspective reveals the shape and color of the object but not necessarily the texture. If we live in the midthird of our body, we look through the midthird of our eyes and see the world with, or as, our emotional capacity. If we are seeing a living form, especially a human being or some other type of animal, this vantage may reveal to us the emotional "feel" of that being. And if we live mostly in our lower body, we will look out through the bottom third of our eyes and see from the vantage of physical sensation, revealing the texture, the tactile feel of the object. When we begin to inhabit our body as a whole, and see as a blend of awareness, emotion, and physical sensation, we see with the whole of our eyes, and we receive a more complete image of whatever we see. And this is true of all of our senses.

Depth of Contact—Visual

Sit facing an object, such as a lamp or a plant. Attune to the quality of awareness in, around, and above your head. Feel that your whole body is made of awareness. Attune to the quality of awareness pervading you and the object. See the object, while attuned to the quality of awareness.

Attune to the quality of emotion in your chest and gut. Feel that your whole body is made of emotion. Attune to the quality of emotion pervading you and the object. See the object while attuned to the quality of emotion.

Attune to the quality of physical sensation, low in your torso and legs. Feel that your whole body is made of physical sensation. Attune to the quality of physical sensation pervading you and the object. See the object while attuned to the quality of physical sensation.

Attune to awareness and physical sensation at the same time, pervading your whole body. Add the emotional quality pervading your whole body—the three qualities blend together. Attune to the rich space of awareness, emotion, and physical sensation pervading you and the object. See the object while attuned to the blend of awareness, emotion, and physical sensation.

You can do this same practice with a living being, such as a tree, or an animal, or a person. This is also a deepened intimacy and a fuller, more vivid knowing of the world around you.

11

Fluidity

For the power of space is inherent in the individual soul
as the true subjectivity, at once empty of objects and
providing a place in which objects may be known.

—Abhinavagupta

Nondual realization is the simultaneous experience of stillness and movement. We know ourselves as the unbreakable, unperturbable ground of being and the ever-changing complexity of the movement of life at the same time.

As the disentangled dimension of fundamental consciousness, we are no longer clamping down on what we feel and know and perceive. To the extent that we have realized this ground, our breath and energy along with our perceptions, thoughts, emotions, and physical sensations move without obstruction through the stillness. Without this controlling grip on ourselves, we become spontaneous. We become more fluid and responsive to our surroundings.

As fundamental consciousness, we are disentangled from the flow of experience and yet intimately involved with it. If you would like to try this out, gaze for a moment out your window or go outside and let yourself observe the activity in your environment. Whether it is ripples on a lake, waves on the ocean, trees or grasses waving in the wind, or cars and people rushing through a city street, let yourself attune to the stillness of fundamental consciousness pervading both your own body and this movement of the life around you. In any moment, the movement will involve varying complex shifts in its shapes, tempos, and directions, and yet each movement will be clearly and precisely etched in the stillness of fundamental consciousness. As this pervasive stillness, our perception becomes more nuanced and intricately detailed. We have become like an open empty vessel in which each moment registers and changes.

The fluidity that we experience as the stillness of fundamental consciousness is nongrasping; it is letting life happen just as it does. But this is not a passive receptivity. Our actions to affect a situation also occur as part of the unity and fluidity of the moment. And we can also choose not to act on our impulse to affect a situation. We are right there, with all of our faculties to guide our actions. The nongrasping of fundamental consciousness is not in any way a paralysis. It is a dynamic dance of whatever is happening within and around us.

Zen Buddhism offers a story to illustrate this point: A Zen master and his students are walking by the side of a river. Suddenly, they see a man in the water, flailing and calling for help. The master dives into the river and saves the man, pulling him to the shore. The students are confused by this. One young monk says to the master, "But you said to be accepting of any situation." The master answers, "He was drowning!"

I love this story because it shows that the Zen master is not bound by rules of behavior or even the expectations of his students. As in many Zen stories, the authentic response to life is valued over any sort of agenda or religious code. As the basis of spontaneity, the nongrasping of nondual realization is also the basis of authenticity.

In previous chapters I explained that inward contact with our body is, at the same time, openness to our environment. Wherever we have inward contact with our body, we are open and available to respond to our environment. This availability is the fluid aspect of nondual realization. Wherever we inhabit our body, we have let go of our grasp on that aspect of ourselves. For example, to the extent that we inhabit our chest, we become emotionally fluid. We have let go of our suppression, our limitation, of our emotional depth and responsiveness.

It may require some inward attunement for us to become aware of our controlling grip on ourselves. This grip is habitual and unconscious.

It is often just in the process of inhabiting our body that we realize that we have been limiting our experience. Many people are surprised to discover that they are capable of even more love, more pleasure, and more mental clarity and creativity than they have previously experienced.

As we let go of our grasp on our perceptions, emotions, thoughts, and sensations, we may also gain appreciation for the unhindered unfolding of our life circumstances. Even if we do not believe in an intelligent, compassionate universe in which everything happens for some good reason, our whole-body access to our own being can help us to trust that we will be able to meet even painful circumstances with strength and clarity.

We may find that it becomes easier to allow our relationships to grow and change, for example, even if that means loss. We still feel our emotional responses to these changes, but we are more open to seeing situations as they really are rather than denying that changes need to occur. Knowing ourselves as the unbreakable stillness of fundamental consciousness can help us accept the flow of life and the way our lives are transformed with the passing of time.

A more subtle aspect of the fluidity that we gain with nondual realization is in the energy dimension of our being. This is the streaming, pulsing, vibrating aspect of ourselves that produces a sense of vitality within our body. When we know ourselves as the stillness of fundamental consciousness, these subtle energy currents also move more freely and deeply through our body.

Many sensitive people grow up experiencing the energy in their bodies and in their environment. As they become more open, this experience can become overwhelming. They may feel a sense of energetic merging with other people so that they lose contact with their own distinct presence in relationships, along with awareness of their own needs and preferences. They may even feel invaded by the energies of other people. However, they can use their sensitivity to attune to the most subtle ground of their being, to the stillness of fundamental consciousness that pervades their own energy currents as well as those of other people.

As fundamental consciousness, we know ourselves as distinct from our surroundings, and yet we can be even more deeply in contact with other people than when we merge with them energetically. We can allow our own energy to flow through us even more powerfully, without feeling overwhelmed by it. We can also receive the vibrations of other people, feeling nourished by those that feel good and allowing those that feel invasive to pass through the unchanging ground of our being and dissipate.

Our energy system is designed on a spectrum from dense to subtle. When we realize fundamental consciousness, we also uncover the most subtle dimension of our energy currents. We experience a very fine vibration everywhere in our body and our surroundings along with the stillness of fundamental consciousness.

The Core Breath practice described in chapter 10 can help awaken this most subtle aspect of our energy system and integrate it with our breath. We can then experience subtle breath/energy everywhere in our body at the same time. Rather than experiencing our breath as a sequence, for example, as a sensation that begins at the bottom of our torso and rises upward or that begins in our lungs and spreads outward, we experience every part of the internal space of our body breathing at once.

This whole-body breath can help us stabilize in our realization of fundamental consciousness. The stillness of fundamental consciousness pervades the whole-body breath/energy without altering it, and the whole-body breath/energy does not obstruct the undivided stillness of fundamental consciousness. In this way, we can live continuously in our embodied realization of fundamental consciousness because we can breathe without disrupting that realization.

The undivided continuity of the stillness of fundamental consciousness within our body also makes the way we move our body more fluid. When we move our arms, for example, or when we walk or dance, instead of experiencing that our bones move at the joints, it feels as if our movements progress along this undivided continuity within our body. In the Realization Process we call this "stillness moving."

The stillness of fundamental consciousness is always full of movement. Although we can feel the difference between the stillness and the movement, once we have realized fundamental consciousness, we do not experience one without the other.

12

Cultivating Fluidity

n the Realization Process, we make a distinction between the dimension of fundamental consciousness experienced as stillness and the dimension of energy experienced as movement, flow, vibration, or pulsation. Here is an exercise to help you experience the difference between knowing yourself as physical matter, as energy, and as fundamental consciousness.

Attunement to Yourself as Physical Matter, as Energy, and as Fundamental Consciousness

Sit upright, with your eyes open or closed.

Attune to yourself as physical matter. Experience yourself as made of muscle, bone, and all of your physical anatomy. It feels like you have just come from the gym, from doing physical exercise, and you can experience your physical structure.

Attune to yourself as energy. Experience yourself as made of streaming, vibrating, pulsating flow. Streaming energy feels something like water flowing through your body.

Attune to yourself as the stillness of fundamental consciousness. Experience yourself as made of the stillness that pervades your body and environment.

The next practice can help you open to the upward current of energy coming from the ground and moving through the internal space of your body to support it. This is an advanced practice and may take a while to experience. Even if you do not feel any movement of energy at first, if you continue to attune to it patiently, you will eventually experience the upward current.

Opening to the Upward Energy—
Standing and Sitting

Stand with your eyes open. Look straight ahead.

Feel that you are inside your feet. Experience that there is no separation between you and the ground. Let your breath adjust to you being in your feet so that your inhale does not lift you up away from your feet.

Feel that you are inside your whole body, including your feet.

Find the points on the soles of your feet in the center of your heels. Balance your awareness of those two points.

Find the points on the soles of your feet right before the balls of your feet. Balance your awareness of these two points.

Open the points on the soles of your feet and receive the upward-rising energy that comes from below you. Let it come up into your ankles. The upward-rising energy is a subtle (thin) current, like a thread of energy. Do not imagine the energy or draw it upward. Just open to receive it.

Find your hip sockets. Your hip sockets are in the depth of your body. From your hip sockets, you can feel the internal space of your upper thighs and your lower torso at the same time. Balance your awareness of the space inside both hip sockets. Allow your hip sockets to settle toward the floor so that it feels as if you are standing in your legs rather than on them. Receive the upward-rising energy in your hip sockets.

Find your heart center in the middle of your chest but deep within the core of your body. Receive the upward-rising energy in your heart center. The energy now comes up from the points on the soles of your feet, your hip sockets, and the bottom of your torso and rises into your heart center.

Find your shoulder sockets. Balance your awareness of the space inside both shoulder sockets. Receive the upward-rising energy in your shoulder sockets and let it flow down to your fingertips.

Find your head center. Let your head center settle toward the floor. Receive the upward-rising energy in your head center. The energy comes up from the points on the soles of your feet, your hip sockets, and the bottom of your torso and rises through the subtle core of your body into your head center. You can also experience it flowing down through your arms.

Let the upward-rising energy continue out through the top of your head. Stay settled within the whole internal space of the body as the energy rises through you. Stand for a few moments experiencing the stillness of fundamental consciousness within your whole body and, at the same time, the upward current of energy moving through your whole body.

Now sit upright in a chair with your feet on the floor. Inhabit your whole body. Find the space outside of your body. Experience that the space of fundamental consciousness inside and outside your body is the same continuous space—it pervades you. Experience that the space that pervades your body also pervades your whole environment. Remain in your body as you experience this.

Find the point in front of the base of your spine at the bottom of your torso. Open that point and receive the upward current. Let it come up through the subtle core of your body to the top of your head and above. You can also feel the energy flowing down through your arms.

Find the points on the soles of your feet in the centers of your heels and right before the balls of your feet. Open those points and receive the upward current. Let the energy come up through your legs and then join with the current coming up from the bottom of your torso and moving up through the subtle core of your body to the top of your head and above.

Sit for a few moments. Experience the stillness of fundamental consciousness pervading your body and environment and, at the same time, the movement of energy rising through your body. The more settled you are within your body (not collapsed, but internally settled), the easier it will be for you to experience the upward-rising energy. This energy is a subtle (thin) current. If you experience a larger "whoosh" of energy, refine your focus on it until you find the subtle thread of energy within it.

When we know ourselves as fundamental consciousness, our breath becomes integrated with our energy system. This means that just as we can feel our energy everywhere in our body, we can also experience that the whole internal space of our body is breathing. This is a more subtle breath than we feel when we bring our breath into our whole body or when we breathe sequentially, for example, beginning the breath in our abdomen and feeling it move upward into our chest. Instead, it feels as if the breath is already there, within our whole body. Our breath feels like a subtle vibration everywhere in our body at the same time. The very subtle breath that we experience in the core of our body when we practice the Core Breath exercise is now felt throughout our whole body.

The following exercise has two parts. The first part is a preparation for experiencing whole-body breathing. If you can easily bring your breath into your whole body, you can skip the first part and just practice the second part of the exercise.

Whole-Body Breathing

A. Sit upright with your eyes open or closed. Inhabit your whole body.

   Experience your breath coming into your nostrils on your inhale and passing out of your nostrils on your exhale.

Now bring your breath in through your nostrils, down your neck, and into your lungs on your inhale, and let your breath release out through your nostrils on your exhale. Practice this until it feels relatively smooth and easy to feel the movement of your breath coming in and out of your lungs.

Bring your breath in through your nostrils, down your neck, into your lungs, and then into your whole body on your inhale. Let your breath release through your nostrils on your exhale. Do this calmly, just filling as much of your body with your breath as you can, easily. Practice until you feel that you can bring your breath everywhere in your body on your inhale and exhale through your nostrils. Do not move with your breath. Remain stable within your body, and feel the breath move through you. The inhale is a filling, and the exhale is an emptying.

It can make you feel lightheaded to suddenly have more oxygen than you are used to. So just practice each step two or three times at a sitting.

B. Sit upright. Inhabit your whole body.

Find your head center. Just being in your head center enters you into the whole internal space of your body. Initiate your inhale within your head center, and release your breath from within your head center on your exhale.

Find your head center and your heart center at the same time. If you can, add in the pelvic center as well. Just being in these core points enters you into the whole internal space of your body. Initiate your inhale from within all three points—your head center, your heart center, and your pelvic center. Your exhale is a release from within all three points.

The breath within the core of your body has a subtle, slightly buzzy vibratory quality. Now let yourself experience this same subtle core breath within your feet. It feels as if the internal space of your feet can inhale and exhale. And then experience this same core breath inhaling and exhaling within your feet and hands at the same time. Let yourself experience the core breath in your legs. And then in your legs and arms at the same time. Experience it in your pelvis, then in your midsection, then in your chest, and then in your whole torso. Experience the same vibratory core breath in your neck and head. This is not an expansion of the breath outward from the core. It is an initiating of the core breath everywhere within the internal space of your body.

Let yourself experience the subtle vibration of the core breath within your whole body simultaneously. The whole internal space of your body is filled with this subtle, buzzy breath. It feels as if the space within your body is "carbonated" with this subtle breath. Although you will still experience your breath move in and out of your nose, it feels as if both your inhale and your exhale occur within your whole body.

Now attune to the stillness of fundamental consciousness pervading your body and environment. Let yourself experience that the stillness pervades your breathing body without interfering with your breath. The breath occurs everywhere in your body without changing the pervasive stillness.

The next practice is an introduction to moving as fundamental consciousness. In addition to helping us experience more fluidly the movement of life within the body, inhabiting our body as fundamental consciousness helps us to become more fluid in the way we move. We move along the undivided continuity of the ground of our being.

Stillness Moving—Arms

Sit, stand, or lie on your back. Bring your arms straight out to your sides, perpendicular to your body. If you are sitting or standing, your palms face straight forward. If you are lying on your back, your arms are lying on the ground with your palms facing the ceiling. Inhabit your whole body, including your arms.

Find your head center. From your head center, find the internal space of both wrists. Balance your awareness of the space inside both wrists.

Inhale by opening your chest to space, as if you could draw your breath into your chest through the pores of your body, bringing your breath into the internal depth of your chest.

Exhale with a *ssss* sound, sending your breath and sound through the internal space of both shoulder sockets, arms, wrists, and hands. Try to make the vibration of the breath and sound equal through your right and left arms. Do this twice. Breathing through your arms in this way can help you open the space within your arms so that you can inhabit them more fully.

Now settle deeply within your arms, wrists, and hands.

Attune to the quality of self inside your whole body, including your shoulder sockets, arms, wrists, and hands. Experience that you are made of the quality of self.

Slowly make a circle with your arms in front of your chest, moving within the internal space of your arms, within the quality of self. The movement begins within the internal space of your fingertips and continues along the undivided quality of self through your hands, lower arms, elbows, upper arms, and shoulder sockets. Feel that the quality of self is moving through space. Your fingertips will almost meet in front of your chest.

Open your arms out to the side, perpendicular to your body (returning to the starting position), moving in the same way, through the internal space of your shoulder sockets, arms, wrists, and hands, moving within the quality of self. You may be able to feel that even though you are only moving your arms, the whole internal space of your body is engaged in the movement.

Repeat moving your arms into and out of the circle twice. Then bring your arms down along the sides of your body and settle within your whole body.

13

Permeability

No longer do finite objects appear as separate and limited
structures; rather, the silent and translucent consciousness
out of which all things are composed surfaces and becomes
visible as the true reality of perceived objects.

—Paul Muller-Ortega

The permeability aspect of fundamental consciousness is generally the most challenging for people to understand. In fact, it
cannot be understood; it can only be experienced. But it is the
defining experience of nondual realization.

We can have an awareness of the world around us that is unwavering. We can feel whole, in the sense of being able to think, feel, and
sense at the same time. We can experience a certain amount of internal depth or depth of contact with other people and with nature. We
can experience the fluidity of energy moving through our body. But
the realization of fundamental consciousness goes further than that.
It is an experience of permeability.

When we know ourselves as fundamental consciousness, we
experience our body as made of consciousness, made of empty
luminous space, at the same time that we experience ourselves as solid.
We also perceive any living or material object in our environment as
both solid and permeable at the same time. This does not mean that
we can actually see through the object or that we can see what is

behind the object but that the object appears to be made of the same expanse of consciousness as our own being.

This is an actual perception. It is not intuition, understanding, or imagination. The medium of this perception seems to be fundamental consciousness itself—the ground of our whole being, including our sensory organs, our awareness, our emotion, and our physical sensation. Fundamental consciousness knows and experiences itself within our body and within our environment.

The Buddhist Heart Sutra states that "form is emptiness, emptiness is form." This phrase is most often interpreted philosophically to mean that all forms are interdependent, that they have no existence of their own apart from their embeddedness in the web of cause and effect. A wooden table, for example, depends for its existence on trees, which depend on earth, and so forth. It is also sometimes interpreted as the emergence of the material world out of nothingness.

However, we can also view the phrase, "form is emptiness, emptiness is form" as a vivid and precise description of the way objects appear when we have realized fundamental consciousness. Everything that we perceive appears to be made of its material substance and the pervasive space of fundamental consciousness at the same time. This is an understanding of the Heart Sutra that can only arise from experience. Like many spiritual texts, the Heart Sutra may offer us this hidden, esoteric meaning in addition to its philosophical interpretations. We look at a tree, for example, and we see the substantiality of the wood, the roughness of the bark, even the vibrancy of its life force. But at the same time we can see and feel that the tree is made of empty space. It is completely permeable, completely empty, in that sense. The same consciousness that pervades our own body pervades the tree. And we have this same experience of both substance and permeability when we look at an inanimate object, such as a table or a toaster. We see the object as a substantial form, and we "see-feel" it as made of consciousness at the same time.

As fundamental consciousness, every aspect of our experience becomes more subtle, more refined. As we let go of the constrictions in our sensory organs and allow the clear open space of fundamental consciousness to receive our sensory impressions, we may access a more subtle range of our senses. We may see light and color emanating from living forms. We may see a web of light and dark lines pervading space. We may hear a very subtle buzzing sound that is finer (thinner) and more diffuse than the sound of electricity.

As fundamental consciousness pervades all of the objects of our senses, our perception seems to permeate beyond their surfaces. Although we cannot actually see the inner content of an object— for example, what a chest of drawers contains—the permeability of objects, pervaded by fundamental consciousness, produces the experience that we are seeing within or through them. With living forms we can sometimes see and feel the life within them. We may be able to see-feel what another person is feeling, or the particular gentle intelligence within a wild animal, or the emotional response not just in the facial expression but within the body of a loved pet. This is one of the most subtle aspects of nondual realization. I will describe it more fully in chapter 15, where I discuss how our realization can transform our relationships.

Since we uncover fundamental consciousness rather than constructing or imagining it, some Asian spiritual traditions have theorized that this unified ground of consciousness is the fundamental nature of the universe. The Hindu Advaita Vedanta claims that all forms are just an illusory superimposition on the true ground of existence, which is undivided pure consciousness. Shankara wrote, "The phenomenal universe of names and forms is falsely superimposed upon Brahman on account of the ignorance of the perceiver."[1]

There is an age-old argument among Buddhist teachers about whether all forms in nature, and even inanimate objects, have this same essence, or Buddha nature, that we can experience pervading them, or whether it is our own consciousness that we are experiencing pervading the world around us. Is fundamental consciousness immanent in all of nature? Or is it our own consciousness, clearly revealed?

Here is another Zen Buddhist story to illustrate this question: A Chinese sage named Daosheng taught that all natural forms have Buddha-nature. When his students and colleagues laughed at his belief, he went out into the fields and propounded his theory to the rocks. The rocks, it is said, nodded in agreement.[2]

If everything really is made of fundamental consciousness, then all forms in nature have this essential ground. However, even if this is true, there is a big difference between having Buddha-nature and experiencing it. In the Realization Process, nondual realization is the experience of ourselves as Buddha-nature. The experience of one's own essence, the realization of our fundamental consciousness, is only accessible, as far as I know, to very conscious forms in nature, such as human beings. Only very conscious species can reach that state in which we are not only conscious but our consciousness becomes conscious of itself.

Although the experience of unified, pervasive consciousness has been described by realized teachers for thousands of years, there is no way for us to know, either subjectively or, so far, scientifically, whether we are experiencing the nature of the universe or our own individual consciousness pervading the objects of our perception. But for the purpose of realization, the metaphysical explanation of fundamental consciousness and its relationship to the phenomenal world is not important. The value of the realization of fundamental consciousness is the great pleasure of our own openness to life, the extraordinary spectacle of a world pervaded by luminous transparency, and the depth of connection and kinship that we can feel with all of nature.

14

Cultivating Permeability

The following practice is meant to facilitate the eventual emergence of the pervasive space of fundamental consciousness and the mutual permeability of yourself and the world around you. It should be practiced daily, if possible, for short periods of no more than ten minutes. It is important not to bring tension to this practice but to sit in a patient, relaxed manner, open to the possibility that you will experience an undivided expanse of consciousness pervading your body and the object in front of you. With practice, the object will appear as permeable, as made of luminous space. This exercise also requires you to have practiced Attunement to Fundamental Consciousness and Core Breath so that you open to the pervasive space with your whole body and being.

Cultivating the Permeability of Objects

Choose an object in your environment and sit upright in front of it with your eyes open.

Inhabit your whole body. Find the space outside of your body, in your environment. Experience that the space inside and outside of your body is the same unified expanse of space. Let yourself experience that you are the space of fundamental consciousness.

Attune to the space pervading you and the object. Sit for a few moments, experiencing that the space that pervades you also pervades the object. Remain in your whole body as you do this. Do not project yourself toward the object but attune to the space that seems to already be there, pervading you and the object.

Sit without strain, patiently waiting for the object to become permeable, for it to appear to be made of space. Sit as long as is comfortable for you. As you continue to practice inhabiting your body and attuning to fundamental consciousness, you will eventually experience the object as pervaded by the same undivided consciousness that pervades your own body.

The next practice can help you experience fundamental consciousness pervading inside and outside your body. This is not a merging with the environment. You are still in your body, and your body still has edges, but they are permeable edges. You are contained within your body and completely open to your environment at the same time.

Cultivating the Permeability of the Body

Sit upright.

Inhabit your chest. Attune to the space within your chest and the space in front of your chest at the same time. Remain within your chest as you do this. Attune to the space within your chest and behind your upper back at the same time. Remain within your chest as you do this. Remaining within your chest, attune to the space within your chest and to the sides of your chest at the same time.

Inhabit your whole body. Remain within your body. Attune to the space pervading your body and the space in front of you at the same time. Remaining within your body, attune to the space within your body and behind you at the same time. Remaining within your body, attune to the space within your body and to the sides of your body at the same time. Remaining within your body, attune to the space above and below you at the same time.

Inhabiting your body, find the space outside of your body, all around you. Remaining within your body, attune to the space pervading inside and outside of your body at the same time.

———————————

Here is one more practice for attuning to permeability.

———————————

Cultivating Permeability Through Movement

Sit upright in a chair with your eyes open.

Feel that you are inside your feet. Let your breath adjust to you being in your feet so that your inhale does not lift you up away from your feet. Feel that you are inside your whole body, including your feet. Straighten your arms and let them hang loosely down by your sides.

Move your arms slightly away from the sides of your body and back down. As you do this, remain inside your whole body, including your arms, hands, and fingers. Use the movement to experience the internal continuity within your arms, hands, and fingers.

Now repeat this same movement but instead of moving the internal wholeness within your arms, let yourself experience your arms as permeable. As you move your arms through space, you can experience space moving through your arms.

———————————

Part 3

THE LIFE

15

Relationships and Nonduality

People sometimes ask me if it is possible to maintain our realization of nonduality in relationships. They ask, "Can there be two people, in relationship, when nonduality means oneness?" The answer is, of course! How impoverished our lives would be if nondual awakening robbed us of the profound enjoyment of relationships.

Much of our life occurs in relationship, in our daily encounters with friends, lovers, family members, and colleagues. Even if we just nod to a stranger we pass in the street, or even if we ignore that person, we are in relation to them. If we could not have relationships in nondual realization, we would not be able to sustain our realization as an ongoing transformation. We would get up from our meditation pillows and as soon as any object or living being came into view we would find ourselves back in duality.

Considerable research has shown that we organize ourselves in relation to other people from the beginning of our lives.[1] We learn the names and purposes of the objects in our world from our earliest caregivers, and we learn to regulate our emotions,[2] to feel safe or unsafe, and to value or devalue ourselves based on our interactions with them. We mimic the way they speak, the way they move, the way they express or hold back love. On the somatic level, we create chronic constrictions in our body in order to limit or block the impact of abrasive or overwhelming interactions with other people, especially when we are children and adolescents. We also create patterns of constriction to restrain any of our behaviors that might evoke parental punishment or peer rejection, and we mirror the design of openness and constriction in our parents or primary caretakers. These protective and mirroring constrictions produce rigidities and fragmentations within our own being and between ourselves and our environment.[3]

This means that even if we can attune to fundamental consciousness on our own, as soon as we encounter another human being, we may reorganize our habitual, protective patterns of self-other fragmentation. For this reason, the Realization Process includes practices for couples, or for any two people, to learn how to relate to each other without interfering with their realization of fundamental consciousness. Although we become less guarded against others as we realize nonduality, we are also less vulnerable. Our deepened contact with our own being makes us more resilient and more able to navigate difficult encounters and to accept or reject the desires and the influence of other people.

FUNDAMENTAL CONSCIOUSNESS DEEPENS CONTACT

When we relate to another person as fundamental consciousness, we can experience our oneness with them and our separateness from them at the same time. Since we are inhabiting our own body, we can keep track of our own needs in a relationship and recognize when we are ignoring those needs or when those needs are not met by the other person. We can know, by experiencing the movement of emotion and sexual excitement within our body, what we really feel for another person and if we are truly attracted to them. The realization of fundamental consciousness can also help us heal our habitual ways of relating with other people, such as our chronic patterns of blocking the vibrations of other people or the tendency to lose our boundaries in relationships.

We can also know in what parts of ourselves we experience contact with another person, and where our contact with another person is obstructed or unavailable. Is it a heart-to-heart connection? A meeting of minds? A mostly sexual relationship? This observation of ourselves, which becomes possible when we inhabit the internal space of our body, can help resolve the confusion and ambivalence that sometimes occurs in relationships.

Contact with another person or with any living being is a difficult experience to describe, but we have probably all felt it. It can be experienced through various aspects of ourselves, including our eyes, touch, and even vocal harmony. It can be felt, for example, as a meeting of emotion, of love with love, as a connection of physical sensation and pleasure with the physical sensation and pleasure in another person's body, or as mutual intellectual excitement. The realization of fundamental consciousness enhances and unifies all of our modes of contact. We can meet and know each other with our whole being. The practices in the following chapter will illustrate this.

By deepening our capacity for contact, the realization of fundamental consciousness enriches our relationships with all other life. The oneness that we experience with our surroundings as this pervasive space is the continuity of the internal depth of our own being with the internal depth of other beings. This experience of internal continuity, of the meeting of depth with depth, means that we can experience contact with another person, or with any form in nature, beyond their surface to the knowing, feeling, sensing being within.

One aspect of this deepened contact with our environment is perceptual—what I have been calling "see-feel." We may be able to see and feel, even across distance, the internal space of another person's body and know, to some extent, what it feels like to be them— the quality of their intelligence, of their emotional capacity, and their experience of physical sensation. We may be able to detect what they are feeling in that moment not by running their emotion through our own body, as many sensitive people do, but by perceiving it over there in the other person's body. Fundamental consciousness pervades our own body and the body of the other person and reveals what we are feeling and, to some extent, what the other person is feeling at the same time. This is a more subtle type of perception than that of entrainment, or mirroring.

People sometimes question whether it is invasive to see another person this deeply. However, we often see more when we observe other people than what they intend to reveal to us, even if we are not attuned to fundamental consciousness. As fundamental consciousness, the perception of the internal experience of another person requires that we remain inhabiting our own body, so we are not intruding energetically into the other person; we are perceiving them across a distance. It is also important to keep in mind that, as with any perception of another person or event, we may be wrong either in what we are seeing or how we are interpreting it.

One consequence of nondual realization is that we become more sensitive to the world around us. While we do not need to curtail our own sensitivity, it is essential that we use our sensitivity with restraint, humility, and compassion in our relations with others.

MUTUAL CONTACT

As I write this, a small bird, a chickadee, lands on a tree branch outside of my window, twisting his head quickly in several directions, surveying his surroundings. I see his form and movement, his muted colors, his alert black eyes, and I see-feel the life, the faint, miniature intelligence within his tiny body. I feel moved in my own heart by my meeting with this tiny kindred spirit. I feel that I am in intimate contact with this bird. However, there is no answering resonance from him. The contact is one way.

This is an intimacy that we can feel with anyone, even someone that we just encounter momentarily in passing. But it is quite different from the mutual contact experienced by two human beings who are both attuned to the pervasive space of fundamental consciousness.

To be clear, we can experience mutual contact with people, and with some animals, even if one or neither being has realized fundamental consciousness. When a cat pushes its head further into a person's stroking hand and purrs, a feeling can pass between the hand and the cat's head that may be experienced by both the human and the animal as mutual contact. Mutual contact between two people who have realized fundamental consciousness is the refinement and magnification of this same experience of mutual contact.

When two people meet as fundamental consciousness, they experience mutual transparency. They feel that they are both pervaded by, or made of, the same single expanse of consciousness. This empty luminous space reveals for each of them their own unique, separate being and their unity with each other at the same time. It endows their contact with all of the attributes of fundamental consciousness—wholeness, steadiness, depth and breadth, fluidity and permeability.

This means that they connect with each other as the blend of awareness, emotion, and physical sensation that is intrinsic to fundamental consciousness. As that unified, unwavering, disentangled ground, they also experience a more subtle range and a freer exchange of energies flowing between them.

They may also experience resonant connection between the essential (uncreated) qualities of their being. These are the qualities that we uncover when we inhabit the internal space of our body. In chapter 6, I named these qualities *understanding, voice, love, power,* and *gender* (or *sexuality*), but whatever we call them, we each experience them in a recognizably similar way. This resonance, for example, of love with love or power with power produces an intensification of these qualities in each person and enriches their contact with each other.

This mutual resonance can also serve as a transmission. If a person is more open to fundamental consciousness in one part of their body than their partner, the resonant contact between them can help their partner open more fully in that part of themselves. For example, if one person has some mild constrictions in their head that prevent their openness to fundamental consciousness in that part of their body, then experiencing the resonance of their own quality of understanding with their partner's quality of understanding can help them release some of their constriction. As a therapeutic method, the Realization Process practices, especially the relational practices, can help people recognize where they need to focus within their body to heal their contact with themselves and others.

The intimacy that we experience with another person as fundamental consciousness does not eradicate our experience of our own being, it enhances it. It enables us to deepen our capacity for emotion, understanding, and physical sensation and to relate to others from that depth. The unbreakable nature of fundamental consciousness also helps us tolerate and remain present for intense emotion and physical pleasure.

As the disentangled, clear open space of fundamental consciousness, we can more easily listen to each other. We can more clearly see each other, more consciously touch each other. We can bond with each other but without grasping, without attempting to hold on to or manipulate the other person to conform to what we want them to be. Just as we can allow the free flow of all our experience, as fundamental consciousness we can allow the people in our lives to grow and to change, regarding even those who are most familiar to us in the clear space of nondual perception each time we meet.

16

Nondual Relationship Practices

Described below are the two main Realization Process practices for two or more people to experience connecting with each other—first as fundamental consciousness and second from the subtle core of the body. You should have some experience doing the Attunement to Fundamental Consciousness and Core Breath practices on your own before doing these relational exercises. Also, it is most important that during these practices you do not leave your own body in order to connect with your partner. The more deeply you can inhabit the internal space of your own body and the core of your body, the more you will experience the depth of contact that occurs when two people are both attuned to fundamental consciousness and both living in the subtle core of their bodies.

Couples Attunement to
Fundamental Consciousness

It is easiest if one of you records these instructions so that you do not have to focus on reading them while doing the practice. **Note that both of you should follow the instructions at the same time so that you are attuning to each other simultaneously.**

Sit upright and facing each other with your eyes open. Do not try to maintain eye contact throughout this exercise, but keep your eyes open so that you are aware of your partner visually.

Breathe smoothly and calmly. Inhabit your feet. Let your breath adjust to being in your feet so that your inhale does not lift you up away from them. Inhabit your whole body, including your feet. Find the space outside of your body. Experience that the space inside and outside of your body is the same continuous expanse of space. It pervades you.

Experience that the space that pervades you also pervades your partner. Remain in your own body as you experience this.

Inhabit your whole brain. Find the space inside your own brain and inside your partner's brain at the same time. Attune to the quality of understanding inside your brain. Attune to your own quality of understanding and your partner's quality of understanding at the same time.

Inhabit your neck. Find the space inside your own neck and inside your partner's neck at the same time. Attune to the quality of your voice inside your neck. Attune to your own quality of voice and your partner's quality of voice at the same time.

Inhabit your chest. Let yourself settle in your chest so that you feel like you are sitting in your heart. Find the space inside your own chest and inside your partner's chest at the same time. Attune to the quality of love inside your chest. Attune to your own quality of love and your partner's quality of love at the same time.

Inhabit your midsection. Find the space inside your own midsection and inside your partner's midsection at the same time. Attune to the quality of power inside your midsection. Attune to your own quality of power and your partner's quality of power at the same time.

Inhabit your pelvis. Find the space inside your own pelvis and inside your partner's pelvis at the same time. (Please skip this part of the practice if it is uncomfortable for you.) Attune to the quality of gender, however that feels to you, inside your pelvis. Attune to your own quality of gender and your partner's quality of gender at the same time. (If you are nonbinary, you can attune to the quality of your sexuality instead or to whatever you feel when you inhabit your pelvis.)

Inhabit your whole body. Attune to the quality of self inside your whole body. Attune to your own quality of self and your partner's quality of self at the same time.

Find the space outside your body. Experience that the space inside and outside your body is the same continuous space. Experience that the space that pervades you also pervades your partner. As that space you can let go of your grasp on both yourself and your partner. Let yourself and your partner be just as you are in this moment. Let the space receive you both. Relax your visual field so that it becomes one with fundamental consciousness, so that it feels like the space is doing the seeing.

The following core-to-core practice is the second of the main Realization Process relational practices. There are several other relational practices, but they are all based on these two. The core-to-core attunement can be particularly helpful if you tend to energetically merge with other people, as it can help you feel deep connection with another person and with yourself at the same time. When you make eye contact with your partner across the distance between you, you may feel that you become farther away from your partner. But this is your true distance. We often pull people toward us with our vision, merge with them through our eyes, or attempt to block them by hardening our eyes against contact. Even though you may feel more space between you and your partner during this practice, you will be able to feel oneness with them when you connect core to core. You may experience a slight vibration, a gentle "buzz" that occurs simultaneously within your own core and your partner's core when you make that connection.

As in the first relational practice above, it is easiest if you make a recording of the instructions so that both partners can easily follow them without having to read them.

Contact Core to Core

Note that both of you should follow these instructions at the same time so that you attune to each other simultaneously.

Sit upright and facing each other with your eyes open.

Breathe smoothly and calmly. Inhabit your feet. Let your breath adjust to being in your feet so that your inhale does not lift you up away from them. Inhabit your whole body, including your feet.

Find your head center. By being in your head center, you enter into your internal wholeness; you have access to everywhere in your body at once without leaving your head center. Staying in your head center, make eye contact with each other across the distance between you—be aware of the distance between you as you make eye contact. From your head center, find your partner's head center. Do not leave your own head center to do this.

Find your heart center. By being in your heart center, you enter into your internal wholeness; you have access to everywhere in your body at once, without leaving your heart center. Staying in your heart center, make eye contact with each other across the distance between you—be aware of the distance between you as you make eye contact. From your heart center, find your partner's heart center. Be careful not to come out of your own heart center to do this.

Find your pelvic center. By being in your pelvic center, you enter into your internal wholeness; you have access to everywhere in your body at once, without leaving your pelvic center. (Please skip this part of the exercise if it is uncomfortable for you.) Staying in your pelvic center, make eye contact with each other across the distance between you—be aware of the distance between you as you make eye contact. From your own pelvic center, find your partner's pelvic center. Do not come out of your own pelvic center to do this.

Find your head center again. Find your head center and your heart center at the same time. Find your head center, your heart center, and your pelvic center at the same time. Staying in all three points, make eye contact with each other across the distance between you—be aware of the distance between you as you make eye contact. From all three points in your own body, find the same three points in your partner's body.

Inhabit your whole body. Find the space outside your body. Experience that the space inside and outside your body is the same continuous space. Experience that the space that pervades you also pervades your partner.

———

Here is a brief attunement to help you experience how contact with another person is enhanced when you both inhabit your own body. We sometimes feel that we will get closer to someone if we attempt to merge with them, but in leaving our own body we actually diminish the contact that we can feel with another person.

———

Deepening Contact

Both partners follow the instructions at the same time.
Hold each other's hands.

Now inhabit your own hand. Let yourself experience how this changes the feel of the contact between you.

In this attunement, you are not sending energy into your partner's hands. You are just holding hands with each other and inhabiting your own hands.

With an intimate partner, you can practice this with any part of your body. Instead of merging with each other, remain within your own body as you touch.

———

Living Nonduality

In the eyes, it is called seeing; in the ear, hearing; in the
nose, smelling; in the mouth, talking; in the hands, grasping;
in the feet, walking. Fundamentally, it is one light.

—Rinzai

Nondual realization is a lasting, ongoing transformation of our whole being. It brings wholeness, steadiness, depth, fluidity, and subtlety to every aspect of our experience. We do not have to make an effort to apply this realization to our daily lives. When we realize fundamental consciousness, it is just there, deepening our receptivity and our responses to the world around us, refining our perception, filling our own being with a gentle sense of contentment, and imbuing our body and surroundings with subtle luminosity.

Nondual realization is usually reached in two main stages. At first we have glimpses of it—moments in which we may suddenly feel that the boundary between our own being and the world around us dissolves, and everything we perceive appears to be made of empty space or light or something we recognize as "beingness," as existence itself.

Then, in the second stage, we stabilize there. We live in and as that subtle oneness all the time. We get used to it. It is just the way life is, just the way we are. In moments of quiet, in nature, in atmospheres of particular beauty, we may find it remarkable again—that same single, subtle light in our own body, in every other living being, in the sky and earth, and even in material objects. An actual oneness, of being whole in oneself but entirely open to and continuous with everything around us.

The realization of nonduality is a radical shift from our usual dualistic experience of life. From a world of separate enclosed forms, we find ourselves in a world without boundaries. Although objects are still distinct in themselves, and there is still spatial distance between objects, there is also continuity that coexists with but transcends these demarcations. Even more extraordinary is the permeability of objects. From a world of separate and distinct substances, such as wood or flesh or water, we find ourselves in a world that is made out of one undivided primary element that again coexists with but transcends these differences. Our own being and the world around us have become permeable, both substantial and made of the radiant, pervasive space of fundamental consciousness at the same time.

The world expands. This is not an inflation of ourselves, not an outward energetic movement. It is an inward deepening that increases our perspective, that opens into an expanded reach of contact and perception. It is an experience of distance and intimacy at the same time. In a dualistic world, it is as if we are cramped in our environment, boxed in and yet shut out. We live at the surface of ourselves, close to the surfaces that surround us. In nonduality, we live in the center of ourselves. We feel and know and sense from the innermost core of ourselves. Paradoxically, our protections against life keep us bound up with it. As we let go of these constrictions and barriers within our body, our world also becomes unbound.

However, even after we have made this shift and stabilized there, we can continue to increase our realization. If you have found the practices in this book helpful, then even after you have stabilized in your realization, you can continue to inhabit your body more fully, to initiate your breath within your subtle core and within your whole body, and to open more completely to the unwavering space of fundamental consciousness. You can still find areas of constriction and remaining fragmentations within your body and release them into the undivided ground of your being. Becoming free, becoming whole, is a gradual, ongoing, lifelong process. My students sometimes feel discouraged when I tell them this, as if they were hoping that I was leading them toward some sort of perfection. But their disappointment is usually short-lived. For with each small letting go, there is an increasing sense of freedom. There is more love, more awareness, more sensation of being alive. There is more emptiness and more presence pervading us inside and out.

NONDUALITY AND PERSONALITY

Nondual realization not only changes our experience of ourselves and our environment, it also affects our personality and behavior. Inhabiting our body helps us feel calmer and more in possession of ourselves, which can help us feel confident. It can give us a sense of belonging, of being at home, even when we are among strangers. This goes a long way toward alleviating social fears.

As fundamental consciousness, we know ourselves as the fundamental, steady ground of our being. Although we still feel pain, we know that we cannot be annihilated by that pain.

We gain self-knowledge. We have direct contact with our responses to the world around us. We know our motivations, preferences, needs, aspirations, and fears—all of the internal movement of our life that makes us who we are and that guides our choices. This can help us aim toward whatever will make us happiest, most satisfied and fulfilled. Instead of attempting to be who we think we should be, we are more able to be who we are.

Knowing ourselves as fundamental consciousness can also help us experience genuine pride, to respect the basic sacredness of our own being. Most of us grow up with some degree of self-doubt. We may strive to believe in our own goodness, to develop self-esteem, but that is not easy to achieve. No matter how many times we tell ourselves or even are told by others that we are valuable, that we are worthy of love and success, the underlying unease with ourselves may persist. In my experience, the most effective way to alleviate this unease and to feel genuine self-love is by inhabiting one's body as fundamental consciousness. It becomes increasingly difficult to dislike ourselves when we actually experience ourselves as radiant, as made of light. It is difficult to doubt our basic goodness and goodwill when we feel our love as a steady presence within our chest, when we notice the spontaneous upwelling of our compassion for other people.

I am not saying that we become saints. Although most people report that they do feel more tolerant of others, we may still have moments of anger or jealousy or dislike for other people. But we are more likely, when we live within our body, to notice these emotions immediately so that we have the chance to understand and possibly resolve them and to react in a more conscious, less destructive way in our relationships. Like good parents, our basic trust in ourselves is not shaken by the recognition of our faults. We can more easily accept ourselves as a whole when we can feel the basic integrity, the authenticity, of the ground of our being.

The pervasive space of fundamental consciousness is a great equalizer. If we hold ourselves above or beneath other people, this holding pattern may obstruct our realization of this mutual ground of being. The experience that we are made of the same fundamental substance, the same light, as all other living beings evokes a sense of kinship with other human beings and with all of nature. Although the Realization Process does not teach a moral code, this sense of kinship can help us behave toward others in a more ethical way.

Many people wonder why, if this is so, supposedly enlightened teachers so often misbehave, abusing their students with unwanted sexual advances, shaming criticism, or financial exploitation. How is this possible? Like many of the questions I am asked in my role as a spiritual teacher, I have no answer for this. I have no insight into the minds of revered teachers. My only explanation is that people are extremely complex, and the realization of fundamental consciousness, even after we have stabilized there, is still relative, and our internal contact with our body is still incomplete. We can continue to hold our deepest psychological wounds within our body and mind that might cause us to pass on our own trauma to others. The practice of inhabiting the body is not only an important component of nondual realization but also of psychological healing. It can help us experience the constrictions in our body where we are not in contact with ourselves and uncover and release the memories and emotions held in those constrictions. And that can help us resolve the beliefs and behaviors associated with them.

SPONTANEITY

The internal fluidity that we experience when we know ourselves as fundamental consciousness is reflected in our behavior as spontaneity. This is not a lack of control or an acting out of impulses that might be destructive to ourselves or others but rather a nongrasping onto ourselves or others. We are present to any situation with our understanding and our compassion. As I have said, we also have our function of agency, which enables us to choose to act or not act, depending on our understanding of the situation. But there is a flow to our interaction with life. We are able to trust ourselves in our wholeness, in our access to our love and our understanding, so that we can let go of our vigilance toward ourselves and other people. When we inhabit our body as fundamental consciousness, we become less self-conscious. We shift from experiencing ourselves as an object for others to appraise and judge to becoming the subject of our experience looking out at the world.

Spontaneity means that we are present to the unfolding of each moment, without preconceptions, without manipulation, without attempting to grasp on to what we like so that it never changes or to eliminate from our perception and understanding anything that we do not like. There is a big difference between approaching life with assumptions and habitual ways of seeing and hearing and actually thinking, actually perceiving. It is like the difference between painting by numbers and actually painting, allowing the painting to evolve on a blank canvas.

NONDUALITY AND GOD

People also sometimes ask me if we can have a relationship with God and also realize nonduality. Since the Realization Process is not a metaphysical system or in any way a religion, it does not affirm or deny the validity of religious or metaphysical beliefs. However, all of our relationships are deepened and enhanced through the realization of pervasive fundamental consciousness. If you have a relationship with God, then that relationship will also be enhanced through the realization of oneness.

Many great dualistic religious teachers have described an experience of God that closely resembles nonduality. The Christian mystic

Meister Eckhart (1260–1328) wrote, "If you want to discover nature's nakedness, you must destroy its symbols, and the further you get in, the nearer you come to its essence. When you come to the One that gathers all things up into itself, there you must stay."[1]

The Jewish mystic, Rabbi Nachman of Breslov (1772–1810) wrote:

> Grant me the ability to be alone; may it be my custom to go outdoors each day among the trees and grass—among all growing things and there may I be alone, and enter into prayer, to talk with the One to whom I belong. May I express there everything in my heart, and may all the foliage of the field—all grasses, trees, and plants—awake at my coming, to send the powers of their life into the words of my prayer so that my prayer and speech are made whole through the life and spirit of all growing things, which are made as one by their transcendent Source.[2]

The rabbi feels nature awaken in his presence. He feels the life within the natural forms, as well as their underlying oneness. This seems to echo Eckhart's description of nature's nakedness and its essence. It also reminds me of a line from the Sufi poet Rumi: "As you live deeper in the heart, the mirror gets clearer and cleaner."[3]

I also appreciate that in his prayer, Rabbi Nachman asks for the ability to be alone. I have described how nondual realization enhances our connection with other people and with all of our surroundings. But along with this gift of deepened connection, it also gives us the ability to be alone. This aloneness is not necessarily the absence of other people. It is the absence of remembered voices, of other people's cautions and criticisms. It is the absence, at least temporarily, of the need for approval, affection, and guidance, of our vigilance to potential dangers to ourselves and even of our vigilance to the needs of others. When we can be alone within our own individual being, in contact with our own being in all of its depth and subtlety, we can be truly in contact with the world around us. When we are in solitary communion with the ground of our own existence, then we are connected to the ground of all existence.

From these descriptions, it seems that nonduality, the oneness of our own being with all being, can be revealed in the depths of prayer, just as it is found in the depths of meditation.

PRESENCE AND EMPTINESS

The Realization Process practices can be used on their own or in combination with your current prayer or meditation practice to accelerate, increase, and stabilize your realization of nonduality. As I have described throughout this book, the realization of fundamental consciousness can be unveiled and experienced in several different ways. We can attune to it as a dimension of perfect balance, of stillness within the movement of life. We can experience it as a blend of awareness, emotion, and physical sensation. We can know it as a blend of the qualities that Tibetan Buddhism attributes to it: emptiness, clarity, and bliss. And we can also attune to it as a blend of emptiness and presence. In the Realization Process, emptiness and presence are not philosophical or metaphysical terms. It is not that objects manifest their presence out of a background of emptiness. Rather, these are tangible qualities of nondual realization.

We can inhabit our body as emptiness so that we feel like an empty vessel. We can feel that we are made of emptiness and that our environment is made of an undivided expanse of emptiness. We can inhabit our body as presence so that we shine from within. We can feel that we are made of presence and that our whole environment is made of an undivided expanse of presence. And we can inhabit our body as a blend of presence and emptiness. We can feel that we are made of this blend and that our whole environment is made of an undivided expanse of emptiness and presence.

People sometimes find it easier to attune to either emptiness or presence. As emptiness we may fear that we will disappear or be too insubstantial to function in our lives. As presence we may fear that we will be too conspicuous or too aggressive toward other people. But we neither disappear nor overpower as fundamental consciousness. We need to attune to both, to experience ourselves as the blend of emptiness and presence, in order to know ourselves as the fundamental, pervasive ground of our being. Although at times we may be more aware of either the emptiness or the presence aspect of fundamental consciousness, they are never actually separate. As fundamental consciousness, we are always empty, and we are always present.

18

Practices for Living Nonduality

I n the Realization Process, our practices of inhabiting our body, contacting the innermost core of our body, and attuning to fundamental consciousness pervading our body and environment help open us to the natural emergence of nondual realization. With consistent practice, we find that we are just there, living as fundamental consciousness.

During the initial phase of nondual realization, however, when you are attuning to fundamental consciousness and when you are glimpsing it and then losing it again, it can be helpful to take your practices out into the world. It can be helpful for both your initial entranceway into nondual reality and for your eventual stabilization to cultivate nondual realization in action.

You can practice while walking down a city street, for example, or standing in a supermarket aisle, participating in a meeting at work, or during an emotionally charged family dinner. In any situation, you can attune to the core of your body, to the qualities of your being, such as your love, power, and understanding, and to the space of fundamental consciousness pervading your own being and everyone and everything around you.

But these real-life practices should be done as temporary attunements, not as static constructions. If you try to hold on to fundamental consciousness or to your core or to any of the qualities of your being, this may become a gripping and cause tension in your body. It will interfere with the subtlety of inward contact and openness that the practices are designed to cultivate. It is best to do the practices of these attunements and then let go of them so that eventually, fundamental consciousness can arise spontaneously. Let yourself dwell in the attunements while interacting with your environment, just as long as you can maintain them without gripping.

Walking Outside as Fundamental Consciousness

A. Stand outside with your eyes open. Breathe smoothly and calmly. Inhabit your feet. Let your breath adjust to you being in your feet so that your inhale does not lift you up away from your feet. Inhabit your whole body, including your feet. Attune to the quality of self in your whole body.

   Walk down a street in a town or city or walk through any public place, such as a supermarket. Remain inside your body and attuned to the quality of self within your whole body as you walk.

B. Stand outside with your eyes open. Breathe smoothly and calmly. Inhabit your feet. Let your breath adjust to you being in your feet so that your inhale does not lift you up away from your feet. Inhabit your whole body, including your feet. Attune to the quality of self in your whole body.

   Find the space outside of your body. Experience that the space inside and outside of your body is the same continuous space. Attune to the space pervading your body and environment at the same time.

   Walk down a street in a town or city or walk through any public place. Attune to the space pervading you and your surroundings as you walk. Experience that you are receiving all of the sensory stimuli—the sounds, sights, and smells—as the pervasive space of fundamental consciousness. The sounds and sights and smells move through the stillness of fundamental consciousness without changing the stillness in any way.

Experience the internal continuity of yourself within your body as you walk. At first, you will probably need to practice walking slowly in your own environment to be able to stay inside your body and attuned to fundamental consciousness as you walk.

C. If you can practice in nature: Stand outside on the earth or the sand with your eyes open. Breathe smoothly and calmly. Feel that you are inside your feet. Let your breath adjust to you being in your feet so that your inhale does not lift you up away from your feet. Inhabit your whole body, including your feet. Find the space outside your body. Experience that the space inside and outside your body is the same, continuous expanse of space. Experience that the space that pervades you pervades your whole environment.

Bring your attention to the earth or sand. Experience that the space of fundamental consciousness that pervades you also pervades the earth or sand. Remain within your whole body as you do this.

Bring your attention to the sky. Experience that the space of fundamental consciousness pervades you and the sky at the same time. Do not leave your body as you experience this.

Repeat this with any natural form in your environment, letting the space pervade you and a mountain, lake, ocean, or any other form. Allow whatever sounds or movement are in your environment, such as the flight and song of birds or the sound of the wind and the waving of branches or grasses or the sound and ripple of waves in water, to move through the unwavering stillness of fundamental consciousness without disturbing your attunement to the stillness.

You may be able to feel that you can drop roots into the earth or sand without moving from within your body and continue to feel those roots as you walk.

If you are in an urban environment, you can still practice attuning to fundamental consciousness pervading you and the sky, the ground, and all of the shapes and movement and sounds around you. We can experience fundamental consciousness pervading concrete as easily as we can experience it pervading earth. And we can drop our roots through the concrete.

The next practice can help you speak as fundamental consciousness. You can begin by practicing speaking to an imagined person, as in the following instructions, and then bring your practice into your interactions with people in real life. This practice can be particularly helpful when you are in conflict with someone. When we inhabit our body as fundamental consciousness, our voice is imbued with all of our human capacities, including our mental clarity, our love, and our power. As this pervasive ground of being, we can also listen more clearly, and we can stay attuned to our basic connection with the other person even during an argument.

Speaking as Fundamental Consciousness

Sit with your eyes open or closed. Breathe smoothly and calmly. Inhabit your feet. Let your breath adjust to you being in your feet so that your inhale does not lift you up away from there. Inhabit your whole body, including your feet. Find the space outside of your body. Experience that the space inside and outside of your body is the same continuous space of fundamental consciousness. Remain within your body as you do this.

Imagine someone from your life in front of you. Make sure that you can stay within your own body and in contact with yourself as you imagine them.

Attune to fundamental consciousness pervading you and the image of the person. You can also attune to the qualities of awareness, emotion, and physical sensation, and then the blend of all three, pervading you and the image of the person.

Let yourself feel your response within your body to this imagined person in front of you. Stay attuned to the pervasive space as you say whatever you need to say to this person. You can also open to receiving a response from the imagined person, as the pervasive space of fundamental consciousness.

Dissolve the image of the person and make deep contact with yourself within your own body.

One of the most mysterious and rewarding aspects of inhabiting one's body as fundamental consciousness is that we have access to a source of happiness within ourselves that is not dependent on circumstances or even on our mood. I am not an advocate of attempting to cover up or ignore what we are feeling, especially if there is some good reason for it. We need to be able to feel and express all of our emotions when they are our genuine response to a person or event in our lives. But if we have ongoing, mild anxiety or we are just feeling a little low, we can always change our mood with the following practice. (Please note that I am not suggesting that this practice can heal severe anxiety or depression.)

Attuning to Happiness

Sit upright with your eyes open or closed.

Breathe smoothly and calmly. Inhabit your feet. Let your breath adjust to you being in your feet so that your inhale does not lift you up away from there. Inhabit your whole body, including your feet.

Bring your inhale down into your chest and let yourself find and breathe into the happiness within your chest. Your exhale can be a release; let the breath go wherever it goes.

Continue to find, with your breath, the happiness within your chest.

Now experience that same feeling of happiness within your hands.

Experience the happiness within your feet.

Experience the happiness within your whole body. Experience that the whole internal space of your body is gently breathing. You are breathing the happiness within your whole body. If your eyes are closed, open them and continue to breathe the happiness within your whole body.

Find the space outside of your body. Experience that the space inside and outside of your body is the same continuous space of fundamental consciousness. Experience that the space that pervades you pervades your whole environment.

Experience the stillness of fundamental consciousness pervading the movement of your breath and the feeling of happiness within your whole body. The stillness of fundamental consciousness does not interfere with the breath or the happiness as it pervades your body.

———————————————

The following is a practice to experience fundamental consciousness as a blend of presence and emptiness.

———————————————

Attuning to Presence and Emptiness

Stand with your eyes open. Breathe smoothly and calmly. Inhabit your feet. Let your breath adjust to you being in your feet so that your inhale does not lift you away from your feet. Inhabit your whole body, including your feet.

Experience inhabiting your body as emptiness, as if you are an empty vessel, as if you are made of empty space—pure receptivity.

Walk through your environment as you inhabit your body as emptiness.

Stand still. Attune to emptiness pervading your whole body and environment at the same time.

Walk through your environment, experiencing your body and your environment as pervaded by emptiness, as made of empty space.

Stand still. Experience inhabiting your body as presence. This is not a shining from the surface of yourself but from within the whole internal space of your body.

Walk through your environment as you inhabit your body as presence.

Stand still. Attune to presence pervading your body and environment at the same time.

Walk through your environment, experiencing your body and environment pervaded by presence.

Stand still. Experience inhabiting your body as emptiness and presence at the same time.

Walk through your environment as you inhabit your body as emptiness and presence.

Stand still. Attune to emptiness and presence at the same time pervading your body and environment.

Walk through your environment, experiencing your body and environment pervaded by emptiness and presence at the same time.

Stand for a moment, experiencing the blend of emptiness and presence pervading your body and environment. Experience that the whole internal space of your body is breathing without interfering with your attunement to the stillness of fundamental consciousness pervading your body and environment as emptiness and presence.

Epilogue

To study the spiritual literature on nonduality is to witness the attempt, across cultures and throughout centuries, to describe a surpassingly odd experience, a body and environment made of undivided, luminous transparency. It is like a sun lighting up an empty sky, says one scripture. It is like a thousand suns, says another. It is like a crystal, an uncompounded sphere that encompasses everything, self-effulgent pure consciousness pervading everywhere. To read these texts is also to understand the extraordinary value that this experience has had for the people who uncovered it. Amazing and wonderful, they proclaim. The most precious gem, a pearl beyond price.

What is precious about this experience? Although it is right here within our own body, to find it is like unearthing a rare treasure. Many books about nondual awakening also use the term "natural" to describe it. They say it is "natural bliss," "natural liberation," "natural heart essence." It is both extraordinary and natural. To know ourselves as the fundamental ground of our being is to achieve the freedom to be who we truly and naturally are—to embody our actual nature of love, of wisdom, of pleasure.

Some seekers may come to nondual teachings to eradicate or transcend their earthly existence and find that they can do neither. But even though, as fundamental consciousness, we are always still here, the realization of this ground greatly enhances our gladness to be here. For the realization of nonduality is a source of profuse enjoyment. It is the pleasure of direct contact with ourselves and our world. This is the freedom of nonduality: the freedom to know and enjoy our existence and to live as the fullness of the ground.

Acknowledgments

First, my deepest gratitude to everyone who is right now on a spiritual path. We share the most profound endeavor. As we steer toward the one light, however we each conceive of that, we find each other.

My heartfelt thanks to my first readers for your support and clarity: Aura Glaser, Roma Hammel, Candace Cave, Marcia Haarer, Christi Bemister, Michael Lydon, and Theresa Scott. And to my brilliant, eagle-eyed editor, Sarah Stanton, and the whole team at Sounds True, who welcome their authors with such warmth. And to Zoran Josipovic—for everything.

Notes

INTRODUCTION

1. *Hindu* is a British colonial term that encompasses several great spiritual traditions in India. I will use it sparingly to distinguish traditions such as Advaita Vedanta, yoga, and Kashmir Shaivism from Buddhism, which also arose in India. It is based on the Sanskrit word *sindhu,* first used by Greeks and then by invading Persians to refer to people living along the Indus River in northwest India.

CHAPTER 1: TWO VIEWS OF NONDUALITY

1. Susan K. Hookham, *The Buddha Within* (Albany: SUNY Press, 1991).

2. Longchen Rabjam, *The Precious Treasury of the Basic Space of Phenomena,* trans. Richard Barron (Junction City, CA: Padma Publishing, 2001), 79.

3. Longchen Rabjam, *A Treasure Trove of Scriptural Transmission: A Commentary on the Precious Treasury of the Basic Space of Phenomena,* trans. Richard Barron (Junction City, CA: Padma Publishing, 2001), 51.

4. Shankara, *Upadesa Sahasri,* trans. Jagadananda (Madras: Sri Ramakrishna Math, 1989), 111.

5. Jaideva Singh, *The Siva Sutras* (Delhi: Motilal Banarsidass Publishers, 1979), 59.

6. Douglas Phillips, "Take a Good Hard Look," *Lion's Roar,* May 13, 2014, lionsroar.com/take-a-good-hard-look/.

7. Khenpo Tsultrim Gyamtso Rinpoche, *Progressive Stages of Meditation on Emptiness*, trans. Shenpen Hookham (Auckland, N.Z.: Zhyisil Chokyi Ghatsal, 2001), 74, 76.

8. Peter Levine, *In an Unspoken Voice: How the Body Releases Trauma and Restores Goodness* (Berkeley: North Atlantic Books, 2010), 287.

9. Keiji Nishitani, *Religion and Nothingness* (Berkeley: University of California Press, 1982), 32.

CHAPTER 2: ARE WE OR AREN'T WE?

1. Douglas Edison Harding, *On Having No Head*, (London: Shollund Trust, 2013).

2. Brahmasutrabhasya, 11.3.7., quoted in E. Deutsch, *Advaita Vedanta* (Honolulu: University of Hawaii Press, 1973), 50.

3. The term *dharma* has several meanings, including the inherent principles or natural laws governing the universe, the teaching of those principles, and living according to those principles. The use of it here refers to the teaching.

4. Irmgard Schloegl, trans., *The Zen Teaching of Rinzai* (Berkeley: Shambhala Publications, 1975), 22.

5. Schloegl, *Zen Teaching*, 30–31.

6. Keiji Nishitani, *Religion and Nothingness* (Berkeley: University of California Press, 1982), 164.

CHAPTER 3: OUR BIRTHRIGHT

1. Circa 200–250 CE.

CHAPTER 4: THE REALIZATION PROCESS

1. Shankara, *Self-Knowledge*, trans. Swami Nikhilananda (New York: Ramakrishna-Vivekananda Center, 1946), 171.

2. Judith Blackstone, *Trauma and the Unbound Body* (Boulder: Sounds True, 2018).

CHAPTER 7: STEADINESS

1. Rainer Maria Rilke, "Autumn," in *Translations from the Poetry of Rainer Maria Rilke*, trans. Mary D. Herter Norton (New York: W. W. Norton, 1938), 75.

2. Seung Sahn, "Universal Substance," Kwan Um School of Zen (website), accessed October 30, 2022, kwanumzen.org /teaching-blog/2019/3/13/universal-substance.

CHAPTER 9: DEPTH

1. Yogapedia, s.v. "sat-chit-ananda," accessed October 16, 2022, yogapedia.com/definition/5838/sat-chit-ananda.

2. Shankara, *Self-Knowledge*, trans. Swami Nikhilananda (Madras: Sri Ramakrishna Math, 1987), 178.

3. Khenpo Tsultrim Gyamtso Rinpoche, *Progressive Stages of Meditation on Emptiness*, trans. Shenpen Hookham (Auckland, N.Z.: Zhyisil Chokyi Ghatsal, 2001).

CHAPTER 13: PERMEABILITY

1. Shankara, *Self-Knowledge*, trans. Swami Nikhilananda (New York: Ramakrishna-Vivekananda Center, 1946), 125.

2. Richard M. Jaffe, ed., *Selected Works of D. T. Suzuki* (Oakland: University of California Press, 2015), 128.

CHAPTER 15: RELATIONSHIPS AND NONDUALITY

1. Daniel N. Stern, *The Interpersonal World of the Infant* (New York: Basic Books, 1985).

2. Allan N. Schore, *Affect Regulations* (New York: W. W. Norton, 2003).

3. For a fuller discussion of this, see Blackstone, *Trauma and the Unbound Body* (Boulder: Sounds True, 2018).

CHAPTER 17: LIVING NONDUALITY

1. Quoted in Thomas Merton, *Zen and the Birds of Appetite* (New York: New Directions, 1968), 13–14.

2. Excerpt from Rabbi Nachman of Bratslav, "Prayer for Nature," sefaria.org/sheets/114332?lang=bi.
3. "Deeper in the Heart by Rumi," Rivers Renewed (website), accessed September 8, 2022, nicodemasplusthree.wordpress.com/2015/08/19/deeper-in-the-heart-by-rumi/.

Resources

Hookham, Susan K. *The Buddha Within*. Albany: State University of New York Press, 1991.

Khenpo Tsultrim Gyamtso Rinpoche. *Progressive Stages of Meditation on Emptiness*. Translated by Shenpen Hookham, Auckland, N.Z.: Zhyisil Chokyi Ghatsal, 2001.

Loy, David. *Nonduality*. Amherst, NY: Humanity Books, 1998.

Muller-Ortega, Paul Eduardo. *The Triadic Heart of Shiva*. Albany: State University of New York Press, 1989.

Nishitani, Keiji. *Religion and Nothingness*. Translated by Jan Van Bragt. Berkeley: University of California Press, 1982.

Rabjam, Longchen. *The Precious Treasury of the Basic Space of Phenomena*. Translated by Richard Barron. Junction City, CA: Padma Publishing, 2001.

Sankaracharya. *Self-Knowledge*. Translated by Swami Nikhilananda. New York: Ramakrishna-Vivekananda Center, 1946.

Stambaugh, Joan. *The Formless Self*. Albany: State University of New York Press, 1999.

Yuasa, Yasuo. *The Body: Toward an Eastern Mind-Body Theory*. Translated by Nagatomo Shigenori and T. P. Kasulis. Albany: State University of New York Press, 1987.

About the Author

J udith Blackstone, PhD, is the founder of the Realization Process, an innovative method of embodied psychological and relational healing and nondual spiritual awakening. She teaches workshops and teacher certification trainings throughout the United States and online. The Realization Process includes practices for realizing and stabilizing in nondual realization, as well as a method of recovering from trauma called Healing Ground, a method of relational healing called Empathic Ground, and a method of embodied movement called Stillness Moving.

Judith was a psychotherapist in private practice for many years and before that, a professional dancer. Her long spiritual path has taken her to numerous teachers, mainly within Zen and Tibetan Buddhist and Hindu traditions. However, the Realization Process practices emerged outside of any traditional lineage in response to her own need for healing and realization and the needs of her students. Her main teachers have been the challenge of healing a severe back injury; the natural unwinding, in meditation, of the body, heart, and mind toward openness; and the emergence of fundamental consciousness. Her books include *The Enlightenment Process*, *The Empathic Ground*, *The Intimate Life*, *Belonging Here*, and *Trauma and the Unbound Body*. To learn more about the Realization Process and Judith's teaching schedule, please visit realizationprocess.org.

About Sounds True

Sounds True was founded in 1985 by Tami Simon with a clear mission: to disseminate spiritual wisdom. Since starting out as a project with one woman and her tape recorder, we have grown into a multimedia publishing company with a catalog of more than 3,000 titles by some of the leading teachers and visionaries of our time, and an ever-expanding family of beloved customers from across the world.

In more than three decades of evolution, Sounds True has maintained our focus on our overriding purpose and mission: to wake up the world. We offer books, audio programs, online learning experiences, and in-person events to support your personal growth and awakening, and to unlock our greatest human capacities to love and serve.

At SoundsTrue.com you'll find a wealth of resources to enrich your journey, including our weekly Insights at the Edge podcast, free downloads, and information about our nonprofit Sounds True Foundation, where we strive to remove financial barriers to the materials we publish through scholarships and donations worldwide.

To learn more, please visit SoundsTrue.com/freegifts or call us toll-free at 800.333.9185.

Together, we can wake up the world.